RIDING ON THE WILD SIDE

RIDING ON THE WILD SIDE

Tales of Adventure in the Canadian West

DALE PORTMAN

VICTORIA · VANCOUVER · CALGARY

Heritage House Publishing Company Ltd.
#108 – 17665 66A Avenue
Surrey, BC V3S 2A7
www.heritagehouse.ca

Heritage House Publishing Company Ltd.
PO Box 468
Custer, WA
98240-0468

Library and Archives Canada Cataloguing in Publication
Portman, Dale
    Riding on the wild side: tales of adventure in the Canadian West / Dale Portman.—1st Heritage
House ed.

ISBN 978-1-894974-80-6

    1. Portman, Dale. 2. Park rangers—Alberta—Banff National Park—Anecdotes. 3. Horsemanship—
Anecdotes. I. Title.

SB481.6.P3A3 2009   333.78'3092   C2009-900073-3

First edition published 2004 by Altitude Publishing Canada Ltd.

Library of Congress Control Number: 2009920307

Series editor: Lesley Reynolds.
Cover design: Chyla Cardinal. Interior design: Frances Hunter.
Cover photo: Comstock Images. Interior photos: Dale Portman, except pages 21 and 58, courtesy of
Don Mickle.

 Mixed Sources
Cert no. SW-COC-001271
© 1996 FSC
FSC

The interior of this book was printed on 100% post-consumer recycled paper,
processed chlorine free and printed with vegetable-based inks.

Heritage House acknowledges the financial support for its publishing program from the Government
of Canada through the Book Publishing Industry Development Program (BPIDP), Canada Council
for the Arts and the province of British Columbia through the British Columbia Arts Council and the
Book Publishing Tax Credit.

 BRITISH COLUMBIA
ARTS COUNCIL
Supported by the Province of British Columbia

 The Canada Council | Le Conseil des Arts
for the Arts | du Canada

12 11 10 09   1 2 3 4 5

Printed in Canada

Dedicated to the memory of Bert and Faye Mickle, Keith Foster, Jim Rimmer, Cal Hayes and Art Twomey, some of whom passed on much too early in life.

Contents

Ya Ha Tinda Bound
Scott Ward

There's a place on the Eastern Slope
In the mountains deep
It's a place of rolling grass
Where the Red Deer River sweeps
I'm riding north into that land
Where silence can be found
I'm riding north, I'm Ya Ha Tinda bound

In Canada the great white north
The bitter cold descends
Alpine passes choke with snow
And Mother Nature sends
A bitter wind down valleys steep
Is running southern bound
I'm riding north, I'm Ya Ha Tinda bound

These ponies they deserve a rest
Been goin' hard since June
Step out son it's not far now
We're gonna be there soon
These horses tend to slip and slide
And skid on frozen ground
I'm riding north, I'm Ya Ha Tinda bound

When I arrive, I'll pull their shoes
And turn 'em out on grass

They will lope out through the gate
They are free at last
When heavy snows obscure the ground
They'll feed on bales round
I'm riding north, I'm Ya Ha Tinda bound

I see the ranch past Warden Rock
As vistas open wide
My pace picks up this is the end
Of a long and cold hard ride
When spring arrives, we'll chase 'em in
And trail them to town
Then after six months work, they'll be Ya Ha Tinda bound

John and Dick and Rob they train
The colts from good ranch stock
They'll gentle 'em and ride 'em hard
'Til they don't shy or balk
And when those colts go to the parks
They'll be good and sound
And after six months work, they'll be Ya Ha Tinda bound

And when I'm old and crippled up
And can no longer ride
I will sit out on my porch and remember vistas wide
And when it's time to bury me
Beneath the cold hard ground
In my mind, I'll be Ya Ha Tinda bound
In my mind I'll be Ya Ha Tinda bound

Prologue

I SAW THE HORSES WE *were chasing enter the timber, followed moments later by Ron, Bert and Donny, riding hard, pursued by a cloud of dust. My horse, Annabelle, and I were on the right course but were some distance behind. The mare reached out, stretching, covering as much ground as possible with each stride as the wall of timber came closer and closer. Although the speed was exhilarating, a fleeting image of the mare tripping in a gopher hole crossed my mind. It was soon pushed aside by a rush of fear as we raced toward the seemingly impenetrable trees.*

I had to slow things down; I needed to see if there were any snags or deadfall lurking in the shadows. No chance—we made the transition at full speed. Everything was black for a second, then my eyes adjusted to the changing light. Branches whipped by. The mare was caught in the thrill of the chase, and all I could do was let her have her head and hope to stay in the saddle.

Annabelle dashed around a large spruce and then thundered toward some deadfall strung between two trees. It was going to hit me chest-high. With one hand on the reins and one hand clasping the saddle horn as an anchor, I braced myself for the collision. The wood was rotten and exploded on impact—miraculously, I was still in the saddle. It didn't take me long to realize that Annabelle had no game plan and was running just for the love of it.

1

Backcountry Bound

THE MILLARVILLE MAFIA IS THE affectionate name given to a group of six individuals who were raised in Millarville, Alberta, during the late 1950s and early 1960s. This wild group of guys spent their early years chasing horses west of Millarville and doing a lot of youthful partying. They eventually settled down, however, and established successful careers in Canada's national parks. Five of the six worked for the outfitter Bert Mickle. Five of the six also went on to work for the warden service, mainly in Banff National Park. I wasn't raised in Millarville, but I worked for the Mickle family and later joined the warden service. This brought the group's membership to seven.

Bob Haney, chief park warden (CPW) of several national

parks in the east, eventually became the CPW of Banff National Park; Perry Jacobson, CPW of Kootenay National Park, took over as the CPW in Banff when Bob retired; and Keith Foster became the CPW of Grasslands National Park in southern Saskatchewan. Donny Mickle, meanwhile, became the cultural resource warden in Banff and spent many years as a park warden in Yoho National Park, while Johnny Nylund, for years a barn boss in Banff, became foreman of Ya Ha Tinda, the government ranch west of Sundre, Alberta.

Dave Wildman was the only one not to pursue a career in the warden service, but he did work for Bert Mickle and was brought up in Millarville. He is now a successful rancher near Sangudo, Alberta, with his spread located on the west banks of the Pembina River.

I joined the warden service in the spring of 1969. The highlights of my career were the 12 years spent as a dog handler and the many trips I made patrolling the backcountry on horseback. All of us had strong ties to the land and our upbringing in the foothills of the Canadian Rockies— and saddlebags of stories to tell about life on the range.

* * *

It was early September 1966, and a cold mist lay over the pony stand like a new fleece cloak as we rode out that morning for Temple Lodge. It had snowed briefly overnight, giving the landscape an airy feel. All I knew was that we were headed for the Skoki country and I was excited to be working in the mountains for Millarville outfitter Bert Mickle. The sun came out as we rode along the old Fish Creek Fire Road, headed for Temple Lodge and the trailhead. Our saddle horses were eager and prancing as we followed a small remuda of horses. Skip took the lead at the trailhead, while I fell in at the rear.

Only a day or so before, Skip Brochu had been hired by the Mickles for the fall hunting season. I got tossed into the mix because I was a friend of Skip's and they needed two wranglers. For me, it was a rare opportunity to see some of Banff's remote backcountry. I was just 20 and had no wilderness experience. Skip and I had chummed around that summer working as Brewster cowboys, taking dudes to the end of the lake and back. I had mastered the cowboy drawl and swaggering walk that were all-important for attracting the chambermaids and waitresses of Deer Lodge and Chateau Lake Louise. Despite these distractions, we were still in need of a change. One-hour rides were kid's play compared to multi-day adventures with pack horses into unknown country. It was time to escape the repetitive daily rides.

Skip and I finally arrived at Temple Lodge late in the afternoon, where we were met unexpectedly by a slightly tipsy Bert Mickle. He was bridling a horse, while his wife, June, and two Millarville cowboys, Bob Haney and Keith Foster, looked on with concern. No one in the yard was impressed with Bert and his parody of "Kid Shaleen" from the 1965 western *Cat Ballou*. Several of us still had to get to Skoki Lodge, and it was getting late. Skip and I corralled the horses and then walked up to the lodge where Keith and Bob were throwing supplies into pack boxes. Bert was sitting on the steps, the cigarette in his mouth held in place by a tanned hand. He was supervising.

We walked over to Bert, and he stood up stiffly, listing slightly to one side (he had a monstrously cranky back) and introduced himself to me. Here I was, a punk kid, shaking hands with one of the toughest-looking men you could imagine. His appearance belied the fact that he had a heart of gold. He wore a stained and dusty Stetson that was originally black, but with all its trail grime, it could have been any colour. The curl on each side was flattened tight to the brim, giving him an eccentric but dangerous look. His long face was worn, weather-beaten and wrinkled, like the hide of an elephant. Big, black, bushy eyebrows shaded his narrow eyes, and his long sideburns came down level with his small, thin-lipped mouth. In the middle was a flattened nose, pasted to his face much like the brim of his hat. I gulped and said, "Hello," my voice squeaking.

Bert, June, Skip and I, and a group of cowboys headed for Skoki that late afternoon with 20 loose horses. On the team were Bob Haney and Keith Foster. They were both from Millarville and were far more experienced with horses than I was. I watched them closely over the next few days, sizing them up, although they paid little attention to me. They weren't unfriendly in any way, but they were about three or four years older than me, which is a big gap when you're only 20. Bob was the serious one and carried himself like he knew what he wanted out of life. Keith, who had worked for the outfit for the past several years, was lively and animated.

The first couple of kilometres of the trail wound through a forest of dark green spruce with patches of downy larch. We came out into an open subalpine meadow and saw a one-room cabin used by skiers in the winter on their way to Skoki Lodge. Built on a prominence overlooking the surrounding landscape, it was called Halfway Hut because it was located midway between the village of Lake Louise and Skoki. Bert called me "kid" as we rode on toward Boulder Pass, and he pointed out the surrounding peaks: Redoubt, Ptarmigan and Pika. Looking back, you could see the sweeping lines of the ski runs and the distant sentinels surrounding Lake Louise—Mounts Temple, Aberdeen, Lefroy, Victoria and Whyte.

Soon, we crested a bouldery crown of land, and there before us was Ptarmigan Lake, my first alpine lake. The trail skirted the shore to the left and then steadily angled up to a pass in the distance. As if on cue, everyone produced a bottle of whisky from his saddlebag. I accepted every offer to take a swig and felt my sobriety begin to wane.

The sight of horses and riders spread out ahead of me was exhilarating as we crossed the meadows heading for Deception Pass. At the summit of the pass, Bert Mickle charged around in high spirits, wielding a long pole like a lance—a western Don Quixote. Before long, Bert had fallen off his horse and everyone was howling with laughter. Bob Haney, disgusted with Bert's behaviour, headed off down into the Skoki Valley, leading the pack horses.

A short time later, I saw a column of smoke above the trees, and then the main lodge at Skoki came into view. Quite a group, including Bert and June's son, Donny, came out to meet us as we rode by to the corrals behind the lodge. It was a lively bunch that sat around the dinner table that night, telling stories and enjoying a few bottles of whisky.

Much later, I woke up in the dead of night in a strange bed. Total darkness filled the room, and I had no idea where I was. I desperately needed to find a way out—my bladder was ready to burst. I groped around for the door and soon realized I was in a small room. I examined every crack and corner until I finally brushed the latch. I stopped. My eyes were slowly adjusting to the scant moonlight, and I could see a pitcher silhouetted next to a slowly materializing window. With relief, I peed into it and then found the bed and went back to sleep.

Next morning, I heard a knock and was up in a flash. I called out that I'd be right down, grabbed the pitcher and dumped the contents out the window. I had the pitcher in my hand as I went downstairs, intending to rinse it in the creek before going to breakfast, but Bert surprised me at the bottom of the stairs as I snuck toward the door. I stashed the pitcher next to a small bookshelf. I didn't want Bert to know that I had used his lovely enamel pitcher with its unique floral design as a urinal. He asked me to bring in some wood for the fire.

When I got back inside, everyone greeted me with barely concealed chuckles and questions about how my head felt. Bob looked at me as though I was a neophyte who had just gone through an initiation. "Get used to it if you're going to work for this outfit!" he said with a laugh. I had drunk too much the night before, and it was all coming back to me now.

Bert asked me to go down to the corral and let Keith and Donny know breakfast was ready. When I got back, I searched madly for the pitcher, but it was nowhere to be found. Quietly, I slipped into the dining room and sat down for breakfast with everyone else. I reached for a slice of toast and then watched in frozen horror as Bert poured himself some juice from a very familiar pitcher. He brought the glass to his thin lips and drank. An expression passed over his face, a delicate hesitation or reflection, more quizzical than anything else—as though he was trying to identify an aftertaste, subtle but distinct. Then, as suddenly as the expression was there, it was gone, and he poured himself another glass. If I admitted to my secret it would be the shortest job I ever had.

Skip headed back to Temple that day, while a small group of us were assigned to trail the horses out to the Siffleur Wilderness for the start of hunting season. Bob and Keith took up the lead; Donny Mickle and I followed, driving the horses down the trail to the Little Pipestone. Shortly after leaving Skoki, we skirted Merlin Meadows on our descent to the Pipestone River. Donny pointed out Merlin's Castle, a rock formation to the right of us, above the cirque that held Merlin Lake. In two hours, we arrived at the Little Pipestone warden cabin and forded the Pipestone River.

It is a pleasant ride up the Pipestone from this point. The trail passes through old stands of Jack pine, dissecting meadows here and there as it wanders close to the river. When we eventually broke out of the trees onto a small height of land, Singing Meadows lay spread out before us. A meandering stream ran through the meadow, clear and blue. Off to the right, across the valley, Singing Falls slipped down a smooth rock face, adding a magical touch to the place. We felt compelled to stop and drink in the surroundings.

Nearing Pipestone Pass, we came upon an old warden cabin and stopped for lunch. The cabin had scratches all over its logs, some deeply furrowed while others seemed fresher. Keith told me that grizzly bears had raked their claws over the cabin while trying to get in.

After lunch, we continued up to Pipestone Pass. The notch of the pass marked our descent into the Siffleur Valley. The undulating terrain of the upper Siffleur is carpeted with soft vegetation sprinkled with small patches of alpine fir. The area is full of hidden pockets and depressions—ideal for concealing the caribou that are known to live here. Sightings, however, are rare. We found their tracks, but the caribou eluded us, likely cooling off away from the flies in the shade of an east-facing snowfield.

Dale Portman on the banks of the Porcupine Lake inlet, Siffleur Wilderness.

Krummholz (small clumps of alpine fir) started to appear around us as we headed down the Siffleur Valley, and we soon came to a trail junction. To our right was Clearwater Pass, its summit rolling back 170 metres above us. We continued down the valley and eventually broke out into an old burn area. Scattered about were young pine trees growing up around the charred deadfall. This was our campsite for the night, offering us a view of Dolomite Valley and the Siffleur Wilderness.

The campsite was called Wildman Camp. It provided

only the basics: running water, firewood and a view. We unloaded the two pack horses and turned them out. It didn't take long to prepare supper, which required only a can opener and some heat, and we settled in. With great glee, Donny reached into one of the pack boxes and pulled out a bottle of whisky, which he swiftly uncorked—in hindsight, much too easily. He tossed the bottle back and took a swig, then spit it out. Without warning, he began to curse his sister, Faye. She had replaced the contents of the bottle with tea. What Keith called her was not flattering, and I was to find out later that there was no match for Keith Foster's mouth in a situation like this. Bob mumbled something about all the Mickles being the same and retired for the night.

Breakfast brought forth yet more scorn. We headed off early with hollow stomachs, as our eggs were only shells that morning. Faye had blown the contents out through holes at each end. Her name came up frequently over the next hour or two.

Later that morning, we arrived at the wide and boulder-strewn Dolomite stream crossing. It took us a while to coax the horses across, but before long we were in a deep, mossy forest. Finally, we crossed the park boundary—a narrow slash up through the trees, perpendicular to the trail. The path we were following meandered through the timber for another three kilometres before breaking out into a small clearing near the start of a seismic road. Bert maintained his hunting camp near here. The eventful trip was almost over.

As the four of us sat around the fire that night, little did we know that we would all follow the same course and join the warden service. Bob would soon be working in Waterton Lakes National Park as a seasonal park warden, while Keith would do the same in Jasper. Donny's career in the warden service would start in Yoho and mine in Lake Louise.

CHAPTER

2

Spring Roundup

MY LIFE AS A COWBOY started when I was 20 years old and
went to work for the Mickle family, but my real initiation,
however, took place six months later. The spring roundup
on the Red Deer River, not far from the Ya Ha Tinda government horse ranch, was two weeks of hard riding over a
lot of rough country.

The first task for the cowboys was catching all the horses
that had wintered on the open range. Then we trailed them
up to Scotch Camp, just inside Banff National Park, where
we would ride some of them down to take the spring buck
out of them. The roundup culminated in a 60-kilometre ride
up the Red Deer River to Red Deer Lakes and then over into
the Pipestone Valley and down to Lake Louise.

Spring Roundup

The first morning, and every morning of the roundup, we saddled up and crossed the Red Deer River. It was swollen from spring runoff, and the horses were forced to swim. It was a cold wake-up call, as we got soaked to our waists sitting on our horses. Once on the far shore, we followed a seismic line perpendicular to the river up a steep hill until we reached the head of a large meadow that stretched south for several kilometres. The four of us—Bert Mickle, Donny Mickle, Ron Hall and I—rode into this expanse with our eyes peeled, looking for signs of horses. I was on a dark bay mare called Annabelle. She was fast, but I knew little else about her.

We soon spotted a herd of horses grazing in the middle of the meadow some distance off. As we moved up on them, they spotted us and started running toward the timber's edge a kilometre away. We broke out in a lope, heading after them. Annabelle took off with the rest of the group, but instead of heading in the right direction, she ran at a 30° angle away from the others, stretching out, happy just to run. I tried to turn her, but she was too headstrong to pull around. Finally, I had to rein her in to a complete stop, turn her in the right direction and then kick her into a gallop. The others were now well ahead of us, but we at least had something to pursue.

I saw the group of horses enter the timber followed closely by Ron, Bert and Donny. Annabelle and I were on the right course but still some distance behind. After entering the trees at full speed and narrowly avoiding being knocked out of the saddle by rotten deadfall, I realized that Annabelle had no game plan and was running just for the love of it. By now we had completely lost contact with the others. I brought her to a stop after a sustained effort. I had lost confidence in this horse's ability to follow the chase.

We rode northward back across the meadow toward camp in an antsy trot. She wanted to run, and I had to work at keeping her reined in. Eventually, we settled into a brisk walk back to the river's edge. I felt like a dismal failure as we swam back across the river. I wondered how the rest were making out.

Back at camp, June Mickle was no help. "Dale, after all that riding, where are the horses?"

"Well, June," I answered wearily, "if I knew, I wouldn't be here now." I glumly cast my eyes toward the fire. Sensing she had touched a nerve, she asked me if I wanted some coffee.

It seemed like a very long time, but it was probably no more than a few hours until I heard horses splashing in the river. The group had returned and had been successful in capturing about 15 head—a good start to the roundup. Everyone settled around the fire with a cup of coffee and went over how the day's events had unfolded. They laughed as each took turns telling his story of the chase. I stoked the fire and made sure there was fresh coffee, listening to the stories with envy.

Spring Roundup

My saddle horse the next day was White Ranger, a leggy grey thoroughbred with a hard mouth and lots of speed, but little else, as I soon found out. Each of us rode off in a different direction to find the horses. Our theory was that once one of us located them, we would report back and put a plan in place to round up the horses.

Ranger and I were working our way up a hill in the timber when he suddenly stopped. Standing quietly in the trees in front of us was a small herd of horses looking like they had been caught in a game of hide-and-seek. Many had the shaggy, thick appearance of a wild horse, but several had the slicker coats of groomed, ranch-bred horses. They started to move off to the right, then suddenly took off. Generally, the strategy was to try to stay with them until they tired and then attempt to herd them in the right direction, but this required the help of a second rider. I knew I was supposed to report back with their location, but that plan lost its appeal as the excitement of a chase grew in my mind. Although the likelihood of being successful by myself was remote, I decided to stick with them and see what happened.

Ranger and I burst into a meadow at the top of the hill only to see the tail end of the herd ahead of us. For some reason, I thought I could rope one of them. But as I looked down for the lariat, I was suddenly swept out of the saddle by a large, overhanging branch. I landed on my backside and saw Ranger racing off ahead. I got up and ran after him as fast as I could, yelling for him to stop, but my riding boots and shotgun chaps slowed me down. Fortunately, the bridle reins were dragging beside him, slowing him down. I continued to yell until I finally managed to get near him and grab the reins. Within seconds, I was back on him and we were streaking over the crest of the hill trying to catch up to the rest of the horses.

I'd never been on a horse that ran so fast. I was riding pretty loose, just trying to stay with him as trees flashed by. We raced madly over the top of a flat, open summit, and then a gully suddenly appeared on the right. Ranger veered wildly to the left, almost pitching me out of the saddle and onto the ground again. Somehow, I managed to hook the toe of my riding boot on the cantle of the saddle and claw myself back into the seat. I grabbed everything within reach—saddle strings, slickers, even bags.

We hit the trees again and eventually caught up to the horses as they rocketed downhill through a stand of poplar. We were bouncing off trees like balls in a pinball machine. Soon, rails started to appear on my right, then on my left. I couldn't believe my luck. These were the long wings of a catch corral, set in place specifically to capture wild horses. I could see the horses bunching up ahead of me as the corral reached out to contain them.

They were now all in the corral, and I thought, "Wow! Bert is going to be proud of me when I show him all the horses I caught single-handed on my first big chase." But the show wasn't over yet. I needed to dismount quickly to slide the rails across the front of the corral to hold the herd, but my horse wouldn't stop. I pulled on the reins as hard as I could, but Ranger had the bit in his mouth, and we plunged forward until we hit the fence at the back of the corral. I looked over my shoulder only to see the horses dashing out of the corral and up the hill. We stood there, the two of us, Ranger's sides heaving and his tongue working the bit in his frothy mouth, while I gaped in hatless amazement. It was over. They had got away. I started to feel the pain in my knees from the poplar trees we had hit on the way down. Later, when we rode up to the top of the hill and started down the other side, I found the spot where I had been knocked off by the branch, marked by my missing cowboy hat.

I met up with the rest of the group later and told my tale of missed opportunity. After a few hours, we ran into the same bunch of horses and were off crashing through the timber again. For Ranger and me, however, the chase was over. He was spent from the morning's run, and we soon lost contact with the group, but not before I lost my hat again. I spent some time searching for it, but never found it. I got a good ribbing from everyone later. We eventually herded the horses into camp and spent the remainder of the day making repairs around the camp. Bert gave me a blue polka-dot cap as a memento of my missed opportunity. I often wore it over the next few years when I chased horses.

A few days later, a couple of friends of the Mickles

showed up—Dave Wildman and Ivor Lyster. They were two Millarville cowboys with lots of horse-chasing experience. Dave had worked for Bert a few years earlier. Ivor was the brother of Gerry (Red) Lyster, a park warden at Red Deer Lakes. The next day, because of the added manpower, Bert decided we would ride down to the Corners forestry cabin and try to round up as many horses as possible on the way through. June decided to join us on the ride, adding colour to the group with her red hat and buckskin jacket. I was still hoping to be of some use on this roundup and had a gut feeling that today would be the day.

Again, we found ourselves riding south through the first big meadow and then entering the timber at its southern end. Two of the group rode off to the left to check out a hidden meadow, while the rest of us continued to ride south through the trees. Before too long, we flushed a few horses out of the bush. Not wanting to push them too hard, we fell in behind them at a gentle trot. Soon they were joined by other horses that just seemed to appear. Almost by accident, we had a small band trotting ahead of us.

We broke into another open meadow, the horses growing in number. Their leader put his head down, bucked a few times and took off. That was the signal for the rest to follow as they madly galloped south. We were picking up horses everywhere. Suddenly, there was a crashing noise to our left and out of the timber came about 20 head of horses and a few bewildered elk, followed by a couple of yelling cowboys. Eighty

From left to right: Dale Portman, Bert Mickle, Donny Mickle and Laurie McChonachy.

horses now spread out before us in a wave of undulating colour as we galloped at full speed toward the Corners. The excitement mounted as we swept forward, followed by a cloud of dust and exhilarating shouts from the trailing riders.

On each side, a rider moved up steadily on the outside, trying to contain the stretched-out herd and prevent any horses from breaking off, directing them all the while toward the Corners. It wasn't necessary, though, as the horses seemed to know the routine. The chase was all that counted now. As we raced over the country, mud and gravel flew past our heads off the hooves of the leading horses. Our faces spattered with mud, we were none-the-less thrilled with the spectacle of racing animals. All that remained was to corral them at the end of the chase. After eight kilometres of hard riding, we saw the Corners. As if on signal, the horses slowed down enough for us to guide them easily into the big corral.

We had captured more than just Mickle horses. We spent some time sorting out the herd and releasing some of the other horses. After a rare opportunity for a lunch break, seldom enjoyed on the trail back then, we began the task of trailing the herd back to our camp on the Red Deer River. Ron and I went up front to lead the procession, while the rest followed up, urging the horses along as needed. We had to set a good pace that would keep the horses moving without bunching them up, while the riders in the rear had to be careful not to push them too aggressively. Crowding them could set them running past us. It was all a matter of subtle judgment, and after a few kilometres the horses started to string out in single file and settle into an easy pace. A pecking order was established that they would adhere to for the remainder of the day.

After 10 days of hard, exhilarating pursuit, we successfully rounded up all the horses and shod a good many of them. We were now set to trail them through to Lake Louise. The next morning saw us leave the Big Horn campsite with 100 head of horses, followed by June Mickle driving the truck with the camp on board. Things stayed relatively tame as we negotiated the winding road leading across the Ya Ha Tinda between our former campsite and the distant mountains we were headed to. But as we entered open country, everything changed.

Once the horses hit the flat, they burst into a gallop. A few threw their heads down, kicking and bucking, and started to charge past Bert, who was in the lead. I could hear him yelling as he rode hard to keep ahead. The whole herd was now in pursuit, fanning out as we tried to keep them flanked. After a couple of kilometres, they finally settled into a nice easy lope along the fire road leading to Scotch Camp, our destination that first day out.

Things progressed well until we neared West Lakes, the western boundary of the ranch. The night before, Bert and Donny had predicted that White Lady, a troublesome lead mare, and her bunch would make a break from the main group, and they did. They were now headed north toward the lakes, while the rest of the horses followed Bert westward. I stayed with the main group, while Donny and Ron rode out to cut White Lady's group off. Soon the main group started to swing north, too, and I rode hard to keep them flanked, while Bert kept heading west with a few loyal supporters. Eventually, Donny and Ron outflanked White Lady's group and bent them westward toward the main herd. Bert picked up his speed and broke into a gallop. With a lot of yelling, I chased the horses back onto the road behind Bert where, once again, they strung out on the trail to Scotch Camp.

Scotch Camp is the staging area for two backcountry warden districts and has a large, well-fenced pasture with a good set of corrals. It's strategically located just off a fire road that, back then, led to Banff townsite, 48 kilometres away. The cabin is an attractive log structure with sleeping quarters separate from the dining room and kitchen area. Jimmy Simpson—the son of Jimmy Simpson Sr., a legend in the Canadian Rockies—and his wrangler, Jeff Wilson, greeted us when we arrived. Both were based out of Num-Ti-Jah Lodge in Banff National Park and were also there to round up horses.

Simpson's and Wilson's horses wintered up near Tyrrell Creek Flats, which sits on the north side of the Red Deer River, just west of the park boundary. Jeff Wilson was Jimmy's packer and spent the summer months working out of the pony stand at Num-Ti-Jah Lodge. When hunting season arrived, he would turn his attention to cooking on those fall trips.

That afternoon, Bert rounded up the colts and fillies and some older horses that needed to be "topped off" every spring. We all gathered down at the corrals to watch Ron Hall ride the buck out of one of the colts. This was a great way to end the day after an invigorating ride from the government ranch, and I was enjoying every minute of it. It was exciting to watch someone else riding a green-broke colt from behind the safety of the fence.

Donny was the next one up. Bert passed around a bottle

of whisky and each of us took a pull from it. I was enjoying a good swig when my perfect day fell apart. Donny was trotting a now-submissive three-year-old around the corral, waving at us like we were spectators at the Calgary Stampede parade. Bert leaned over the fence, looked at me and said, "All right, kid, you're next." A knot of fear formed in my throat. I thought this show was for experienced hands only, and that I was just a spectator. But there was no escaping Bert.

The first horse I climbed on bucked me off, leaving me dusting myself off and chasing him unceremoniously around the corral. I climbed back on and rode him until he quit bucking, which seemed to take forever. My shirt hung outside my blue jeans as I rode the second colt. As the horse kicked skyward, I felt a tug on my shirt, and most of the buttons popped off like a zipper. I was bounced around all over that saddle as the colt worked out his pent-up energy. On one or two occasions, I came down well forward of the saddle and considered myself fortunate that I didn't land smack on the saddle horn. Magically, I stayed on him and even earned a round of cheers from my whisky-drinking audience. I rode a couple more horses, and by the end of the day I was pretty sore from the pounding I had taken in the saddle and from the rough bounces on the ground.

Thinking back, the day's events are a blur of adrenalin, excitement and whisky. I suppose I passed some sort of initiation test that day, but that was the furthest thing from my mind at the time. More importantly, I had survived. I received pats on the back for making it an entertaining afternoon—it certainly had been for everyone but me.

A lively night followed. Everyone sat around the table swapping stories as bottles of rum and whisky appeared from various duffels. Bert and Jimmy were old friends, and Jeff knew everyone there, except me. I sat back and watched it all, and after such an eventful day, I was the first to hit the hay. I woke up early, about five in the morning, to feed and water the horses in the corral. Jimmy Simpson, Jeff Wilson and Bert Mickle's brother-in-law, Norm Smith, were still up, sitting around the table with a nearly spent bottle of Hudson's Bay overproof rum. It was parked in the middle of the table, attracting them like moths to a light.

In those days, the relationship between outfitters and park wardens was a lot closer than it is today. There was little backpacking activity in remote areas of the park, outside of the odd mountaineering party attempting to bag a faraway peak. The outfitters spent their summer in the park and were an extra set of eyes and ears for the district warden. This mutual association also provided a natural stepping stone for anyone who wanted to start a career in the warden service.

Having taken care of the horses, I came back to the cabin and rousted everyone out of bed. The rest of the horses could be seen out in the middle of the meadow. After breakfast, we rounded them up and headed out. We trailed the horses through to Lake Louise, a distance of 60 kilometres. It was the start of another great summer in the mountains.

3

Born to Ride

EVERYONE SHOULD HAVE AT LEAST one horse in their life. Some people are fortunate enough to have many, but there is always one that stands out. For Donny Mickle, it was Ben.

Donny's first childhood memories were from the original family homestead, Mission Valley Ranch, near the Elbow River, west of Calgary. From there the family moved to their new ranch west of Millarville in the rolling foothills of southwestern Alberta.

Donny's parents always had horses around the place, so he always had something to ride. Neighbours would sometimes say, "Bert, why don't you get rid of those horses and get something useful—like cattle?" But they still kept the horses, as if destiny was playing its hand. Donny's mother,

June, believed that gentle horses were the best babysitters for her children, so Donny and his sister, Faye, acquired many interesting equine friends early in their lives.

Faye's first horse, May, was a hairy little bay mare that kept her company for most of the day, like a devoted companion. It was always interesting when the two small children would try to mount the horses. They would lead them to the corral, climb the rails and crawl onto their backs from this perch. Donny and Faye had found out that if the horses were allowed to shuffle away from the fence, they couldn't reach their objective. As a result, they took turns pushing one horse against the corral while the other climbed on. Then the already-mounted warrior would push the second horse's rear end against the rails while the other rider got on. Because of this, they usually rode bareback around their land, and Faye would sometimes even sleep on May's broad back.

Donny's first horse was Midget; then he graduated to Glassy, aptly named for a white eye that looked like it was made of glass. Mounted on the backs of May and Glassy, the children would race across the hayfields or wander through the heavy timber of the forest reserve bordering their land.

Once, when Donny was about 10 years old, his school buddy, Glenny, stayed for the weekend. After much pleading, Faye reluctantly let Glenny ride May. The boys immediately began galloping around with their cap guns in hand, playing cowboys and Indians. As Donny relates, "I took aim at 'Black Bart' coming out of the trees and fired my cap gun.

Suddenly, I found myself sitting on the ground in front of Glassy. He stood glaring at me with his glassy eye and blowing from his flared nostrils." Later, at dinner, he told this story to his dad. Bert laughed and told him that he had the same problem when Glassy was a young horse. Years earlier, he had been riding along and had shot a deer from the saddle—never a wise thing to do. Glassy immediately blew up and bogged his head. Bert was bucked off with rifle in hand. Glassy, according to Bert, had no use for gunfire from that point on. That ended the gunplay around the OK Corral.

Many of the Mickle's older horses were harnessed to pull the horse mower or the dump rake in the hayfield. The family spent hours raking up freshly cut hay in the hot sun and dumping it in rows to wait for the horse-drawn sweeper. The occasional wasp nest would be stirred up in this fashion, which often turned a tranquil day into chaos as a friendly old horse became a wild runaway.

Each summer, after the hay was cut, baled and stacked, the family would ride west into the comforting mountains of the frontal range. Bert had a trapline in the forest reserve near the North Sheep River (now Threepoint Creek). He had built a log cabin along its banks, and the family spent their summer holidays there. From the cabin, they would take pack trips farther into the deep reaches of the mountains and camp in the many remote meadows that were scattered through the valleys like green emeralds. There was always lots of wildlife to observe and fish to catch in the creeks. Bert loved to hike the ridges and glass for game, so it was natural for Donny to be equally at home riding or walking.

One summer, when their parents returned home early to finish the haying, Faye, Donny and a friend of the family, Elaine Bateman, were left by themselves for a few days at the cabin. They spent their time catching fish and picking berries to enhance their meagre larder, which was fast running out. On one occasion, Faye crept up behind a partridge while it watched Donny, but all she caught was tail feathers. On another adventure, the three of them rode about eight kilometres to their favourite berry patch but found a black bear enjoying himself there, forcing them to make a hasty retreat and leave the berries for another day. There were all kinds of things to keep the children occupied, and at the same time they learned self-reliance.

June and Bert finally returned with more food, just when the children were down to their last box of good old Kraft Dinner. The next day, all of them packed up the necessary gear, food and camping equipment and rode to the Muskeg. This was a large open area spread out beneath the foot of Forgetmenot Mountain, which had a canyon on its south end. There were a lot of wild horses in the area in those days, and they rode past old horse traps along the way. As they rode by, Donny could tell his dad was thinking about his glorious past, chasing wild horses. Although he didn't know it at the time, Donny would find himself back there a decade later trying to catch some of them with his dad. Later that day, they saw a cougar and a bear together near their camp-site. This was a cherished sighting, for cougar are nocturnal animals and rarely seen. Seeing the two disparate animals together was indeed a rare sight.

One of their day rides took them up to the fire lookout on Forgetmenot Mountain, where they visited Curly Sands, the fire-lookout ranger and an old family friend. In his sub-stantial arsenal of stories, Curly had some fascinating tales that captivated a 10-year-old girl and a 12-year-old boy for hours. They even thought some of them were true.

The family spent many wondrous summer days riding, fishing and walking high on the ridges to view the abundant wildlife and surrounding country. It was a special time and place for all of them, but especially for Faye and Donny. It was with reluctance that they finally left this incomparable mountain landscape and returned to their home in the foothills.

More horses came into their lives as the years passed. The family eventually moved farther into the mountains to Banff National Park, where they became guides and outfit-ters. By then, their herd had expanded to about 100 head, and Donny can still remember the names of some of the special ones: Doll, Deuce, Chico, Blue, Jiggs, Pick-Pocket, Jitterbug, Annabelle and Amigo were just a few of them.

In 1964, Donny met Ben, a four-year-old running quar-ter horse from Tip Johnson's stock. Tip was a well-known horseman who had a string of quarter horses, including his stallion Tip Top McKue. Tip was Donny's step-grandfather, and he had passed away earlier that year.

Donny's grandmother was kept busy selling off Tip's many horses, but she kindly said that Donny could choose one of the colts. The horses were pastured at Don Thompson's ranch east of Black Diamond, so Donny went there to look at the four colts in his corral. Three of them were registered quarter horses, and Ben was a grade horse with some thoroughbred in him—commonly referred to as a "running quarter horse." His sire was Tip Top McKue. He was a rangy-looking bay with wide-set eyes that looked at Donny cautiously through a shaggy forelock.

Don Thompson, a good friend of Tip's and a noted rancher and horseman, could see that Ben had caught Donny's eye. He told Donny that Ben had been ridden a few times and that he was Tip's favourite, even though he didn't have papers. He was just what Donny wanted, and they soon had him loaded up for the trip home. After leading him into the corral, Donny gently placed his saddle on Ben's back, put a light snaffle bit in his mouth and stepped into the stirrup. Ben seemed well broke, and as Donny settled into his seat, he realized the horse was also broke to rein.

He was riding Ben around in the corral when Faye arrived on her horse, Gypsy. She was now 19 and had been riding in the forest reserve that bordered their land, looking for her old saddle horse, May. She had been searching for a band of wild horses that she thought May was running with.

May was now in her mid-30s and had had a knack in the past for opening gates, slipping out and joining the gypsy band. At her advanced age, she had been easy to catch, but she'd often taken some of the Mickle horses with her on her escapades. This made for many interesting chases trying to get them all back. The year before, Faye had finally retired the old mare by turning her loose to join her friends in the hills. It was a kind gesture of freedom and a salute to May for being such a loyal friend and companion to her. After all those years, it was good to see her again out there on the range with all the other wild ones.

Gypsy, her new saddle horse, was a high-headed, dark brown mare that Faye was very proud of. She was fast and could easily outrun anything that Donny had been mounted on lately. Faye looked at Ben in the corral, his head hung low sleepily, and commented that her new horse might wake Ben up if they had a race. Donny told her that Ben was young and just getting his legs under him, and he didn't want to run him very far, but he accepted the challenge. They were both surprised to find that Ben loved to run. He left Gypsy like she was standing still, but it took a while before Donny could locate the brakes. The fence was getting close before he managed to turn the horse enough to slow him down. This was one problem he never totally overcame in the many years they were together.

Faye was a little disappointed when she found out she didn't have the fastest horse. Donny didn't gloat, but he wished he had at least made a bet. She felt a little better when he offered her the use of his car to go to a movie in Turner Valley with her friends. She had her own pickup truck, an old Ford that she had inherited from Tip, but the clutch was burnt out and she didn't have the funds to fix it. Tip, who had been on horses all his life, was not the world's greatest driver and was famous for riding the clutch. Faye had been working at the Sunshine ski area in Banff National Park the previous winter and had earned some money, but a new saddle had taken priority over a new clutch. It would be a few weeks before the family started to round up the horses for their new guide and outfitting business and she would finally have some money coming in. Donny had also just returned from spending the winter in Rogers Pass, learning all about snow and avalanches.

The family's involvement in the new business came about from a chance encounter. Bert and June had gone to visit Bert's brother, Jack, and his family in the Columbia Valley of eastern BC. They stopped at Lake Louise to visit an old family friend, Ray Legace. Ray had run the Lake Louise guide and outfitting business for many years and got to know Bert years earlier when he wintered some horses on the Mickle spread in the Mission Valley near Cochrane. Bert and Jack were often enlisted to break the new colts over the winter.

In the early 1960s, when he saw Bert again after many years, Ray was convinced that he had found the right family

Donny Mickle on Ben.

to take over his outfitting business. He even offered to stick around and travel the trails with them to get them started. The Mickles were excited about this new adventure and raised the money for the business by selling some land in the foothills.

Donny started riding Ben every day to get him hardened up for their annual spring roundup. The family always kept a few horses in good shape for the event. In the fall, at the end of the season, they would turn their horses out on a forestry lease near the Ya Ha Tinda Ranch. There they wintered on the abundant montane grasslands near the eastern boundary of Banff National Park. This beautiful open country allowed the ponies to roam the hills with unlimited freedom, so that by spring they differed little from the "wildies" that inhabited the same land. This meant some hard riding to gather them up for the summer work.

This was accomplished during a two-week period in late May and early June while they camped on the banks of the Red Deer River adjacent to the Ya Ha Tinda Ranch. Once gathered, the horses were trailed through the eastern portals of Banff National Park to begin summer work at Lake Louise.

Donny acquired Ben a few weeks before they were due to head for the Red Deer River. He was beginning to take the seemingly gentle horse for granted, thinking that he had him completely under control, but Donny soon realized that Ben was only under control when he wanted to be. This became very clear one morning when he threw the saddle on but failed to notice the tightness of the horse's sides as he adjusted the cinches. When he was reaching for the breast collar, there was a huge and hairy explosion in front of him. Suddenly, there was nothing where the horse had stood a split second before. Ben bucked so hard that the loose stirrups were clapping together over his back like they were applauding him on. I suppose it was Donny's unique perspective from a low vantage point under the fence, but he swears that an entire spruce tree was visible under Ben's belly. The horse bucked, roared and farted across the pasture and back again, then suddenly stopped in front of Donny. He seemed to be grinning as Donny crawled out from under the fence and stood up, still holding his hat on his head. He now gamely mounted Ben, and they trotted away as if nothing had happened. It was a while before he took Ben for granted again.

One day, Faye and Donny rode out to the nearby hills. Their west gate opened out onto an endless expanse of wilderness before touching the slopes of the frontal range. It was only a few kilometres from their gate to the top of Square Butte, a prominent ridge that stretches for miles north and south. From their vantage point on top of the butte, mounted on Ben and Gypsy, they could look over the tree-covered hills that led to the frontal ranges of the mountains. It was a spectacular panorama, from Allsmoke in the south to Banded Peak in the north. All of a sudden, Faye looked down in the valley and spotted two riders. They were leading a familiar horse and winding their way through the aspen forest situated below their vantage point.

Faye, of course, wanted to ride down to meet them. It was Ivor Lyster and Ernie Sylvester, two local cowboys who had been out chasing wild horses. Following along with a rope around her neck was old May. Ivor said they had been chasing a band of "wildies," and he managed to rope the last one as the rest galloped into the trees. He was a little surprised when he discovered the old mare was halter broke and obediently followed them home. Faye stepped off Gypsy and parted some hair on the rear of the old mare to show the boys the Mickle brand. They seemed a little embarrassed when Faye turned the old mare out again. May trotted happily back toward where she had last seen her mustang friends. Ivor and Ernie were well known in the area as wild and daring riders with a reputation for their horse-chasing skills, but Faye was not above teasing the boys about their catch this day. As a matter of fact, she was renowned for her teasing and the many tricks that she played—especially on vulnerable young men who were lured into trying to impress her with vague courting behavior that never did accomplish the misdirected goal.

After weeks of preparation, it was finally time for the spring roundup. The gang crammed camp gear, food and tack into an overloaded pickup truck. A few saddle horses that had been conditioned for the big chases were loaded into the stock truck. Among them was a young Ben, who proudly stepped into the truck along with his more seasoned travelling mates.

It was a pleasant surprise to finally break through the dark spruce forest and come upon the lush green grass and rolling hills of the Ya Ha Tinda Ranch. The road now contoured its way along an open, curving hillside, while the Red Deer River carved its course adjacent to the dark green timber that dominated the south side of the valley. To the west was a gap in the mountains known as Warden Rock, a prominent sentinel that guards passage to the heart of the Canadian Rockies. The mountains, still snow-covered in June, rose in the distance above this sprawling and rolling grassland.

At their chosen campsite near Big Horn Creek, they unloaded the horses and looked warily at the high water of the Red Deer River. The snow melt from the high country on top of the typical June monsoons often made for hair-raising river crossings on horseback.

There were eight of them busy setting up camp and preparing for several days of intense horse chasing that would culminate in the long and exciting ride through the mountains to their summer home. Bert Mickle was there to keep everyone organized and to act as the chief cook for the camp. Bert was a true westerner who had spent his life making a living from the land. He had the trained eye of a veteran who knew how to track whatever quarry he was after. He was always ready to pursue one more adventure, and his enthusiasm usually rubbed off on his family and close friends. Bert would often lean over the big kettle above the fire with ash hanging precariously from the end of his roll-your-own cigarette. Ash regularly seasoned the contents of the pot.

Two girls were on the roundup that year. One of them,

of course, was Faye, who wouldn't miss a roundup and the opportunity to play tricks on the boys. The other was Patty Cooper, a tough, wiry girl who could hold her own in any cussing exchange or fighting match with her male counterparts. She had a fiery temper and gave the boys ample opportunity to test her fragile patience. If there was ever a duelling couple, it was Patty Cooper and Keith Foster, who also possessed a razor-sharp tongue.

Keith was a skinny, bow-legged little cowboy from Millarville who could rattle off a staccato torrent of cusses and insults in a record amount of time. He usually wore a wide-brimmed hat, but because he didn't want to lose his new black Stetson, he wore an English-style derby for the roundup. The comical look of his new hat provoked unflattering comments from the rest of the group, which Keith responded to with enthusiastic rebuttal.

The other hands on the trip were Dave Wildman, Roy (Smokey) Adams and Ron Ecklund. Dave was the tall, dark, good-looking member of the crew. He was also one of the Millarville boys, raised west of town. He managed most of the work on the family ranch after the untimely death of his father. Dave had worked with Bert in the mountains the previous summer and was helping out on the roundup this year before resuming his busy ranch life. It was a break for him, and he loved the sport of chasing wild horses for all its excitement, risk and hard riding.

Roy (Smokey) Adams was a young Cree man who had

spent a lot of time over the years with the Mickle family. Smokey, Bert and Donny had spent the last couple of years making a living cutting posts and rails in the area. Faye and Smokey were also the best of friends. In many ways he was like another brother to her. For one thing, she had long dark hair, soft dark eyes and a dark complexion. Smokey, in fact, looked more like Faye's brother than did blond, blue-eyed Donny.

Ron Ecklund was fresh out of high school, but was already a seasoned horseman and an excellent rider. His parents ran a horse-training business at Elkana Ranches near Bragg Creek, west of Calgary. Ron wanted some experience working with horses in the mountains, so he had signed on with Bert for the summer.

At the campsite, Faye and Patty were setting up their tent when Keith pretended to accidentally trip over their rickety crosspole, bringing the whole thing down on the girls. This set the stage for the remainder of the trip: the war was on.

That evening, Donny and three others decided to take a ride across the Red (the Red Deer River) and up the hill on the far side. Many of the horses would be grazing on the high meadow known as the Ribbon Creek Flats, and they wanted to see how many horses were close at hand in order to plan the chase for the next morning. As they swam their horses across the main channel of the river, they could see the island and its two large, round corrals. This was where they would hold the horses in the following days. There was another large corral about 18 kilometres south on the Panther River. Most of the horses ranged in the area between the two corrals, making for long and exciting days. As they had no camp at Panther River, any horses trapped in the corral there would be trailed back to the Red Deer River corrals,

They successfully rounded up the first group of horses off Ribbon Creek Flats and in a couple of hours were back in camp. Among the horses brought in was Peanuts, a brown mare that Patty liked to ride. Keith was still proudly wearing his derby as he handed Patty the halter shank with Peanuts on the other end.

They sat by the fire with a few beer in hand and exchanged stories of their first chase. Dave and Bert had been able to wing six head of horses down the line when suddenly Keith had come crashing through the trees on Pick-Pocket, a gritty little bay gelding, with two more strays. From there, they had managed to get them all in the corral. Donny told a story about chasing Two-bits, a rangy black lead mare that was exceptionally crafty, and sailing over the cliff into the river with Ben. After a couple of beer, the river became much deeper and the cliff more vertical. The rain had finally stopped and the river was receding as they turned in for the night.

Morning came quickly and the rain held off, but there were dark, ominous clouds forming to the west. After breakfast, the riders crossed a much friendlier river than the night before. To give Ben a rest, Donny was riding Jiggs, a husky dun gelding. Jiggs wasn't too speedy but he was strong, sure-footed and steady. The eight of them approached the edge of the big meadow and saw about 30 horses scattered across the flats. They split up and kept cover just inside the edge of the trees on either side of the small prairie. It was important for them to get around the horses before they were spotted. Once alarmed, the horses would head for the thick timber on the south end of Ribbon Creek Flats.

They got about two-thirds of the way around the meadow before being spotted by the keen-eyed Annabelle. She put her ears down and started toward the forest with a few of her companions. The riders started racing across the flats and through a swampy gully, trying desperately to cut them off.

Faye was galloping full out on Snuffy, a big black gelding, when he suddenly tripped and did a somersault with Faye underneath him. They both disappeared from sight in the wet gully. Donny's stomach turned to ice water, and he rushed over as fast as he could. He was greatly relieved to see Faye and the horse slowly getting back on their feet. Amazingly, they both seemed okay, just muddy and wet. After wiping mud from her saddle and herself, Faye was soon back on Snuffy and ready to go.

The fall left the two of them out of the chase for a while, but Dave, Smokey, Ron and Keith had managed to beat the herd to the trees and turn them back toward the river trail. Bert and Patty rode ahead to wing them near the north edge of the meadow in case they tried to make a break. Donny and

Faye caught up with the group in time to wing the other side of the herd down the line to the corrals. The trip down the hill with the herd running ahead of them was accompanied by a lot of exuberant hollering, laughing and cheering. It looked like they had almost half of the horses in the first two days. This jubilation, though, would be short lived.

There were now 40 head of horses in the two corrals. They would be pastured for most of the day, then recorralled again that night. After changing their saddle horses, some of the riders drove the herd across the main branch of the river to the open valley east of Big Horn Falls and let them graze for the day. Faye, Patty and Donny were put on the first grazing shift, while Dave, Smokey, Ron and Keith went back to look for more horses. Bert went off to the Mountain Aire Lodge with the truck to meet a journalist who wanted to photograph the roundup.

The gap through the mountains known as Warden Rock seemed more inviting than ever. Donny was anticipating trailing the horses through this historical route to the heart of the Rockies. A former hunting ground of the Stoney people, it now lay stretched out before him on this peaceful day. He admired the light green velvet of the mountain prairie, bordered by the darker green of the spruce forest and a backdrop of shining white mountains. The horses grazed peacefully, satisfied with the lush spring grass. For Donny, it was reassuring to hear the loud cowbell on old Two-bits, as everyone wanted to keep a close eye on her.

The sun finally came out while he sat watching Ben graze with his saddle on and his reins dragging on the ground. A slight breeze tussled his hair and softly caressed his cheeks, keeping the early mosquitoes at bay. A few clouds floated by, and the wildflowers were starting to populate the hillside. A sense of well-being coursed through his mind, and he allowed it to linger for a while as he dozed off.

He woke up suddenly. Something was different. Then he realized quickly what it was—he could no longer hear the sweet sound of a noisy cowbell. He cursed and jumped on Ben to have a hasty look around. As a sickening feeling rose in his stomach, he scanned toward the river. The sly old mare must have sensed that she could seize the moment to make her escape. He raced over to Faye and Patty, who were watching the main herd, and yelled that Two-bits had escaped and he was going after her. He couldn't hear their response, but he could guess that some of the language may have been less than ladylike. Donny headed toward the river and soon picked up the horses' tracks to the west off the main trail, following an elk trail that headed south. The potential for a long day lay ahead of him, but he was determined to not come back without Two-bits and her little group in tow. If he didn't catch them, he would have to face the indignation of his companions around the campfire that night and would never live it down.

As Donny made his lonely trek toward the Panther River, Smokey, Dave, Ron and Keith were trailing a small but important band of horses that included the lead mare White Lady. They had managed to trick her by using a snare in a little trap that they had set up on the trail leading into the jungle of timber on the south end of Ribbon Creek Flats. It had taken careful planning to capture the old trickster, but now they were returning to camp triumphantly. Donny was headed in the opposite direction, deflated but determined.

While Donny's shortcomings were being discussed by one and all, a stranger rode in on a rather chubby, sway-backed sorrel mare. He was dressed in pressed jeans, a colourful red shirt and a new straw cowboy hat, held at a jaunty angle. A red silk bandana completed his "drug store" look. Around his neck swayed a cheap Brownie camera.

The stranger announced that he was the journalist who Bert was supposed to meet with the horse truck at the Mountain Aire Lodge. Bert hadn't shown up, so the journalist had ridden all the way along the gravel road to the horse camp. He stiffly dismounted from his horse and then employed his best cowboy shuffle toward the campfire, where he helped himself to a cup of coffee from a simmering ash-filled pot. It didn't take long for the crew to realize that this so-called famous journalist that Bert referred to was probably not sent by any well-known magazine such as *Western Horseman* or the likes. They also correctly deduced that Bert had probably got tired of waiting for him to show up and had driven to town to indulge in a few beer with his buddies in the Sundre Hotel.

Meanwhile, Ben and Donny trotted steadily to the Corners, located 18 kilometres south of their main camp, where the Panther River meets the Dormer River and Dogrib Creek. He had eventually lost the horses' trail in the bush along the way and decided to keep heading south. Two-bits didn't stick to any of the trails, but from past experience Donny knew where she was most likely headed. He arrived at the Corners corrals just as Al Johnson was setting up camp to round up Erving Strom's horses. Erving owned Assiniboine Lodge, near the south end of Banff National Park. Al and a few riders from Banff had come to gather the horses that would be used to take clients and supplies into the lodge that summer.

It was starting to get busy even in those remote parts. Another outfitter, Bill Martin, also had about 50 horses that wintered in the same area, and he would soon be moving in to gather them for his stable in Banff. Bill often bragged that he could shake a can of oats and all his horses would come running to the corral. Bert would often follow this with his own comment: "If you shook a can of oats it would be like a gun going off, and Martin's horses would head for the high timber at full speed."

Donny rode up to Al and asked if he had spotted a sneaky black horse with a bell on her neck, along with two bay geldings and a grey mare. Al grinned and said, "I take it old Two-bits gave you boys the slip." Her notoriety was well known. One of the other riders came up and said that

Doing the dishes at roundup camp, June 1964. From left to right: Dave Wildman, Donny Mickle, Keith Foster (wearing his derby hat) and Ron Ecklund.

he thought he heard a bell down the Panther River a way. This puzzled him because it was not her usual stomping ground, but on the other hand, Two-bits was unpredictable. He thanked them and rode down the river until he came to a narrow trail called the Hand Out. It was well named, because you had to have your hands out in front of you to get through it, and never at any faster than a walk.

Ben and Donny were making their way through this thick, spiny pine forest when fresh horse tracks and some droppings started showing up. They continued following the tracks until Ben stopped suddenly and his ears perked up. Donny noticed and listened intensely. Above them in the deep timber, going the opposite direction from the tracks they were following, was the faint tinkle of a bell. He immediately recognized it as the same sound he had been listening to when he dozed off earlier that morning. He cut straight uphill toward the sound and came upon Two-bits so swiftly that she didn't have any inclination or time to run away. Before she reacted, he reached over and grabbed the bell strap around her neck. She had tried to double back while he was following her in the other direction, the crafty old mare.

After the long ride back to camp, Donny put Two-bits and her friends in the corral and noticed that White Lady had joined the world of captured horses and been similarly adorned with a large and noisy cowbell. He then headed across the river to camp.

When Donny arrived at camp, he found his attention being drawn to the round dude with the straw hat. He was about to ask about him when they all noticed the stock truck winding its way along the hill toward camp. Bert rolled in and was none too steady when he stepped out of the truck. Always thinking of his stomach, Keith wasted no time in inquiring what Bert had brought back to eat. "Barley sandwiches," Bert replied, as he hauled out some cases of beer. One case had been broken open and sampled, indicated by a few empties that rolled out onto the ground.

The dude walked over to Bert to shake his hand, and with a fake southern drawl stated that he was the independent journalist who was coming to write a story and take pictures of their roundup. Bert looked him up and down and said, "Where the hell were you when I came to pick you up this morning?" There was a long, sputtering explanation, devoid of any southern accent, about hiring someone to truck him to the Mountain Aire Lodge and getting lost on the way there. He and his little mare had been dumped off at the lodge. He'd inquired as to where the "roundup lodge" was, and a fellow who manned the pumps pointed up the road, telling him that his accommodation was 28 kilometres up yonder.

After they found out the journalist had only the clothes on his back and a little Brownie camera as possessions, Bert handed him a beer and told him he might as well make himself at home. The dude said he had better picket his horse first and reached into his saddlebag and pulled out a little net. He then wandered around and soon found a rock about the size of a baseball, put it in the net and tied it to the horse's front foot. He drawled on, his accent fully recovered, about how he'd read about this type of picketing in a book about trail horses. They watched in silent amazement as he took off the saddle and turned the little mare loose. She happily started to graze but then suddenly noticed the strange contraption tied to her foot. Her eyes grew wide and buggy, and then she jumped sideways, spooked by her own loud fart and slapping her front paw at this thing hanging from it. As she got all snuffy and charged around amongst them, the rock flew out of the net, much like David's slingshot, and narrowly missed the Philistine's head. Now having very little weight on her foot and nothing holding her back except the net, she tore off and headed into the timber, leaving everyone in the clearing shrouded in stunned silence. This was followed by the extended mirth of cowboys rolling on the ground in varying stages of what seemed like either apoplexy or strangulation.

Dave, the first to compose himself, mounted up and went after the mare, while Bert dubbed the stranger with his new nickname for the duration of his stay: Fish Nets. They then all headed for the campfire to eat whatever was in the stewpot and do some damage to the beer supply. The journalist suddenly took on a humbler persona, his western drawl becoming more urbane as he sipped his beer.

After dinner, the girls decided that they were going to town to have a shower and get more supplies—not from the Sundre Hotel, but from a real grocery store. This was met with rare approval, given the diminishing choices in the larder. Some wondered momentarily at the girls' deceptive smirks as they drove off, but that was soon forgotten as a new round of beer made its way through the crowd.

Bert sat down and rolled a cigarette as everyone took turns telling him of the day's many events. They settled in to talk about their plans for the next day, the conversation interrupted only by the ritual of sipping beer and the nodding of heads. They finally decided they would head back to the Corners to look for the remaining horses, while Keith, Ron and Bert would be put on grazing detail. Two-bits and White Lady would be tied to trees and fed hay. Bert told Fish Nets that he could ride with them the next day, but he should start gathering up horse blankets and tarps to sleep on that night for there was no linen provided at this lodge.

As everyone worked on what remained of the beer, the clouds started rolling in. Brilliant flashes of lightning and deep rolls of thunder were followed by a rain-drenched night. They retreated to their tents, and Keith was the first to crawl into his sleeping bag. He let out a loud yell and curse as his toes slipped into something wet, cold and gooey. He jumped out of his bag and ripped it open to find it stuffed with fresh horse manure. It was a precursor to what the rest of them found. They smelled bad enough without the added aroma now coming out of their sleeping bags. Bert was the only one not affected by the girls' revenge. All of them had to face the rainy night with added adversity as they dumped their bedrolls and tried to wipe them clean with their dirtiest shirts. Donny drifted off to sleep dreaming of various forms of revenge suitable for this latest injustice inflicted on their male domain.

The next morning, Dave and Smokey put Fish Nets and his little sorrel mare between them as they crossed the turbulent river. Both horse and rider were wide-eyed as they bobbed along between the experienced cowboys. After leaving the river, the riders headed up the hill and trotted across Ribbon Creek Flats and on toward the Corners. By the time they had crossed the large meadow, Fish Nets and his horse were played out. He was left to follow as best he could, while the rest moved toward the Panther River at a fast trot.

The group ran into Al Johnson and his riders near the Corners. Donny told Al that if he spotted a wet pilgrim wearing a straw hat and a red bandana and riding a tired little sorrel, that he should tell him to wait at the Corners corral for the rest of them. Al replied that from their description he would probably have no problem recognizing him. Dave mentioned that he answered to the name of Fish Nets.

Al also mentioned that some of their horses had been spotted up the Panther close to the fall hunting camps, so the group set off in that direction. Eventually, they spotted about 20 horses up on an open hillside above the Panther River. Once they surrounded the horses, they headed them back toward the Corners corral.

Smokey was on a horse named Bugs, acting as a wing man on one side. Donny winged the other side, riding Ben, who seemed to instinctively know when to head the horses off and succeeded in thwarting their escape attempts several times. The herd was starting to slow down as the riders moved toward the corrals, but then another group of horses came out of the bush and joined the main herd. Now all of the horses were racing with renewed energy. The new bunch were Bill Martin's horses, and suddenly there were about 40 horses blasting toward the Corners corral. As they broke out into the last flats before the corral, all of the riders were covered with mud from the flying hooves. Suddenly, the Martin horses broke for the Dormer River, but Smokey quickly turned them back into the herd again.

Al Johnson and one of his riders then helped wing the speeding mass as they quickly approached the corral. They were almost there when they spotted Fish Nets and his little mare wandering toward the corral. The two of them suddenly looked up in shock as the thundering herd quickly engulfed them and they became part of the stampeding mass. The horses hit the wings of the corral at full speed. Predictably, both Ben and Annabelle had lost their brakes, and both saddle horses and their riders ended up in their midst, almost chasing the horses back out of the corral. Annabelle and Ben skidded to a halt in the mud just before hitting the rails. Fortunately, Smokey and Al, trailing in the rear, were quick enough to close the gate before the herd could turn and race out. Dave and Donny and their two heaving saddle horses were now captured with the rest of the herd.

Donny looked over to one corner of the corral, where Fish Nets scampered over the rails to safety while the little sorrel mare looked terrified. Donny hollered over at him that he should have some good action photos from his vantage point. Fish Nets looked down just as a large hoof stepped on his Brownie Star flash camera and ground it into the mud. After they had separated Martin's horses, Johnson commented, "It looks like Martin's right about that crazy Mickle outfit chasing his horses all over the country."

Once the herd was in the corral and a few of the lead horses haltered, the steeds finally settled down and considered themselves captured. They were now ready to trail out in a more controlled fashion than they had entered. Donny wondered what to do with the annoying Fish Nets, but Al Johnson came to their rescue and offered to escort him down the Panther River back to the Mountain Aire Lodge and out of their lives. Everyone jumped at this generous offer, and even Fish Nets looked relieved that he had seen the last of them and the Red Deer River country. Donny and Bert never heard from him again, and Donny remembers hoping that the guy would choose a future occupation not related to photojournalism.

Faye and Patty had returned from Sundre and were busy preparing a hot supper of juicy steaks and baked potatoes. They were almost forgiven for what they had done to the sleeping bags. There were reluctant murmurs of thanks for the dinner, but Keith couldn't help but describe in colourful terms what it felt like to slide his feet into a bag of wet horse shit. Faye responded by saying that he always called them fart sacks, "so why not take it to the next level?"

When everyone went to their damp bedrolls that night, the river was lapping at the top of its banks. In the middle of the night, Bert woke everyone. His fear was that the river may have flooded the corrals on the island between the two channels. They quickly decided to bring the horses across the river while it was still feasible. Dave saddled Annabelle, and Donny had enough faith in Ben by now to trust him in swimming water. Dave and Donny decided to ride upriver where Big Horn Creek came in to give them enough room to drift onto the gravel flats on the island. The rest of the crew would be waiting downstream on the camp side to help as the horses crossed.

Ben and Annabelle stepped into the swollen torrent and immediately began swimming. They drifted through the dark water toward the island. The river seemed strangely silent in the void of night. In midstream, a stick drifted close by. It went out of sight and then suddenly rolled over to become a large tree. It narrowly missed them as it twisted down the inky torrent. They could hear the air passing through the horses' nostrils like bellows as they stretched in their effort to gain the dark outline of the far shore.

Water flowed over Donny's saddle and around his waist for what seemed like an eternity. Finally, it started cascading over his cantle and into a backwashed vacuum on the downstream side, exposing his thigh. It told him that Ben's feet had finally found purchase under him, and they slowly gained the far shore.

When they made it to the island they found the water close to the corrals, which held more than 70 nervous horses. Donny immediately opened the gates, and the two of them attempted to herd the horses back across the river to the other side. It was a challenge to push the horses into the raging flood on such a dark night. Survival was uppermost on their minds as they had no idea where they might drift to on the other side of the river. If they drifted down too far, they would enter a stretch of the river that was undercut and steeply banked on both sides. Once carried there, they would be in serious trouble as their saddle horses became increasingly exhausted and panic began to set in.

The last horse finally plunged in and was captured by the current when they heard yelling downriver as the first horses came out on the other side and were picked up by the invisible riders. Somehow they all made it across—even a yearling colt that had struggled to swim at the side of its mother. The horses were left to graze on their own for the remainder of the night. There was no worry about them heading back across the river. As usual, Two-bits and White Lady were fed hay and spent the night tied to a tree.

The next morning, Bill Burrows, the Ya Ha Tinda ranch boss, rode down to the camp to tell them that some of their horses had been seen across the river near West Lakes. This was good news because it was the last of the herd still missing. West Lakes is part of the government ranch and about eight kilometres west of the ranch buildings. The horses were probably hanging out in a large meadow just across the river on the south side.

Bill climbed into the truck with Bert, and they drove ahead to let the riders know where the horses were. Donny, Smokey, Faye and Patty soon had the last 20 rounded up and headed back with the lot. They celebrated with the rest of the beer before June drove into camp that night. The hard riding was over now, and the group focused on trailing the horses back to Lake Louise, following the Red Deer River through Banff National Park.

* * *

Besides being a trickster to all the cowboys who worked for the outfit over the years, Faye was an accomplished poet who often wrote of her love of nature. Her first poem, written when she was 15, was entitled 'Life,' and it showed a maturity well beyond her years. Faye passed over from cancer at the age of 35, much too early in life. In all, she wrote over 100 poems, and many of them are in a book that June keeps close at hand. Her death came a little over a year after her father passed on. Their ashes were scattered together near a plaque that bears her epitaph, the poem 'Life.'

Life

We live to laugh . . . and live to cry.
We live to live . . . and live to die.
We live through happiness and pain,
We live through sunshine and through rain.

God gave us life to love and share,
To help each other and to care.
Life . . . one word . . . so please don't haste.
Life . . . four letters . . . not to waste.

CHAPTER

4

Annabelle
Goes AWOL

BACK IN THE SUMMER OF 1962, the Mickles were in the process of buying Timberline Tours and learning the country, the horses and the business operation from the old mountain man Ray Legace. Not only were they buying an outfitting business, but also the leases to a couple of lodges owned by Sir Norman Watson. Sir Norman was from Britain and the owner of the Lake Louise ski area. The leases included the famous backcountry lodge at Skoki and Temple Lodge. Temple was at the end of the road on the back side of the Lake Louise ski area, conveniently situated at the trailhead for the Red Deer Lakes and Skoki country.

That summer, Donny was a blond, wavy-haired youth of 19. Tall and lean, he fit confidently into his surroundings.

He worked at Skoki Lodge, learning what he could of the country from old Ray. He cut wood and hauled water for the cooks, jingled horses in the early hours of the morning, helped guide the clients who used Skoki as a base for their trips, and travelled the country.

One of Donny's jobs was to pack customers into Skoki on horseback and take them on day trips out of that venerable lodge using the small herd kept there for that purpose. Every morning, he would round up the horses that had been turned out the night before. It was not practical to keep a large amount of hay at the lodge, so each night bells were fixed to the horses and they were let loose to forage for themselves.

Ray had between 80 and 100 head of horses that were scattered between Skoki, the pony stand in Lake Louise, Temple and Point Camp—18 kilometres up the Pipestone River from Lake Louise. Point Camp was where Ray kept the horses that were not being used or those that were infirm or simply in need of a rest from the trail. It consisted of a small tent camp with a corral located next to a huge meadow. Here, the horses roamed freely in the open grassland.

One morning at first light, Donny, along with fellow wrangler Richard Regnier, went down to the corral to get their saddle horses. Three horses had been kept in that night, one of which was Donny's saddle horse, Annabelle.

Annabelle loved to run. Not for any particular purpose, but just for the pure pleasure of running. She was a leggy, dark bay mare of medium build. She had a narrow, irregular white blaze on her handsome face that accentuated a finely featured head. Annabelle was also an unusually intelligent horse and would have made a fine saddle horse if she could only have given up her wild urge to run. That said, she was still a good mount for a rider with a firm hand.

The two blurry-eyed wranglers saddled their horses in silence. They mounted quickly and rode off, shivering in the cool morning air as they hunkered down and headed toward Merlin Meadows, a kilometre below Skoki. Little was said until they broke out into the meadow. There was no sign of the horses, but there were fresh tracks heading farther down the valley. Donny quickly realized the worst had happened—the horses had managed to break through the drift fence during the night and were headed down the valley. Another three kilometres along the trail was a meadow where Donny hoped the horses might have stopped to feed before pursuing their quest for freedom. Sure enough, the delinquent horses stood in the middle of the meadow. As Donny remarked later about Annabelle, "She was a nice horse, but as soon as she got whiff of chasing something, she was totally uncontrollable."

As if by signal, the horses stopped feeding and looked up at the two forlorn riders. Richard and Donny approached cautiously, trying to circle around to the left of them. They wanted to station themselves between the horses and the direction they were headed. It didn't work. The horses bolted and the chase was on. Richard and Donny madly tried to cut them off, but the horses had too much of a lead. They were quickly into the trees and running hard. As Donny followed into the woods, he saw a low branch directly in his path. He tried to pull Annabelle up, but there was slim hope of that. She had already picked out a route directly under the branch. She drove Donny straight into the bony limb, which swept him out of the saddle and onto his backside. Donny remembers being momentarily knocked out and getting a big bump on his head. The last he saw of Annabelle was her rump undulating in pursuit of the rapidly disappearing horses. She never looked back. Donny got up and brushed himself off. There was nothing to do but start walking back to Skoki.

He hobbled into the lodge, and there was Ray sitting in the kitchen with all the guests. Now, old Ray was famous for his lisp. When he saw Donny, he exclaimed, "Jethus Donny. What did you do? You've lotht your horthe and thaddle and you look like hell! Now, I think you're going to be riding thkin ath [skin ass or bareback] for a while." He added, "You better take old Midnight. Yeth, you've done very well, Mithter Mickle."

Donny got little sympathy, and a few hours later, Richard returned with most of the horses; but there was no Annabelle. Richard had last seen her running crazily through the bush, past all the horses and headed in the direction of the Pipestone Valley. Donny climbed on

Bert Mickle

Midnight, the only horse left in the corral, and headed in the direction the horses were last seen. He was riding bareback and had little in the way of food and no concrete game plan, but he'd had enough of Ray's sarcastic wit and was concerned for Annabelle's well-being.

For two days, Donny rode with little rest and only a

quick meal as he occasionally passed by Skoki. He covered all the surrounding countryside, all the meadows and favourite horse haunts, but had no luck. Then, on the third day, he found himself down in the Pipestone. In a meadow just east of where the trail from Skoki reaches the Pipestone Valley, he found a piece of rein from his bridle. Annabelle had been here for a while at least. He headed for Point Camp, six kilometres downstream, to see if she had been drawn there by the presence of the other horses.

At Point Camp, Donny met Bert, who had heard of the missing horse by "moccasin telegraph" and come up to look for Annabelle as well. Donny was relieved to see Bert—he was someone who had chased many a wild horse in his younger days and was quite a bushman and a good tracker. Soon they had parcelled up the country they would each search. Since they didn't have any food with them, they spent some time trying to catch a few bull trout in the river.

With no fishing rods or line, they tried to stun the fish by throwing rocks at them, and eventually caught a couple of fish. They found an old enamel plate, built a fire and cooked the fish for lunch. They then separated, Bert heading up the Pipestone, while Donny rode toward the Red Deer Lakes country adjacent to the Skoki area. That was the last they would see of each other for a while.

Donny returned to Skoki that night, where he expected to meet Bert before heading off to Red Deer Lakes the next morning. When Bert didn't show up, Donny left early the next day on his own, bareback again on old Midnight. After checking out the meadows around the lakes, he headed downstream 12 kilometres toward Horseshoe Lakes. At the Sandhills warden cabin, he met district warden Gerry (Red) Lyster. Red eyed Donny up and down.

"Why are you bareback on that old pack horse?" he asked with a frown on his face.

"I've ridden four days, looking for my horse and my gear," Donny answered, filling him in on the details.

"Well, there's no horse sign around here," Red said. He tied off the diamond on top of his pack horse and then swung up into his saddle and rode off with a grin on his face. "I guess riding bareback ain't all that bad. But if I spot your horse or saddle, I'll send a message out to your dad."

In the meantime, after Bert and Donny parted company, Bert headed up the Pipestone Valley to check out a long string of open meadows beside the river. A couple of kilometres past the warden cabin, where the Little Pipestone enters the Pipestone River, he found a fresh horse track on the trail. Bert was riding an old horse called Chico. Chico was like a bloodhound and had a reputation for tracking horses. He was a popular horse to keep in at night and ride in the morning when you went looking for your "cayuses." He would sniff the ground and then take off in a trot, and you just hung on until he found them. Many a horse turned out for the night has looked up in disgust the next morning on seeing old Chico approach.

When Bert found the track, old Chico bent down and sniffed the black earth. His nostrils flared fully and he snorted hard, like a bellows on a flame. He lifted his head and looked up the valley. Without further ado, he headed out in a slow easy trot to cover the 18 kilometres to Pipestone Pass. Bert kept his eye to the ground. The fresh horse droppings were encouraging. It didn't look like the horse they were following had ever stopped to eat.

When Chico and Bert reached Singing Meadows, they stopped to look around. There was no sign of Annabelle, so they kept riding. Chico never hesitated—he had a job to do and a track to follow. The horse travelled at a steady trot, and Bert was impressed with Chico's new-found energy. The countryside went by with considerable ease.

They reached the old Upper Pipestone warden cabin marked with grizzly-claw scrapes on its logs, but there was still no sign of Annabelle. Finally, they broke out of the trees four kilometres from Pipestone Pass. For a moment, Bert thought he saw the silhouette of a horse on the skyline of the pass, but he wasn't sure. Even uphill, Chico's pace didn't slacken, until finally they crested the summit. There was Annabelle, looking wild and crazy. She stood there, trembling in terror as if the first misstep would send her off on another panicky run. There wasn't much left of the saddle on her back. It was perched precariously in place, held by the rear cinch that had slipped back and was now flanking her. The stirrups, front cinch and breast collar had been stripped off by her close encounters with the trees, as had her bridle.

Bert approached on Chico, ever aware that Annabelle could bolt at any moment. As they drew close, she swung with lightning speed, kicking Chico in the chest. Chico didn't even flinch, and again they approached. Suddenly, Annabelle bolted, forcing Chico and Bert to follow in pursuit. As she ran across the pass, Chico came up behind her. Annabelle cocked her leg and fired again, kicking Chico in the shoulder and narrowly missing Bert's leg. Bert swung Chico around and managed to cut Annabelle off. She came to an abrupt halt. Carefully and with a soothing voice, he dismounted. He spoke to her for a long time with that same soft voice and eventually managed to get within arm's reach.

He started by slowly touching her chest and trembling shoulder as he talked to her. Concealed behind his back in his other hand, he held several loops of a rope. Annabelle was coiled like a spring, quivering, but she stayed where she was. She seemed to understand that all this was necessary. Slowly, he worked his hand up her neck until he was standing next to her. In a comforting tone, he whispered placating noises as he carefully moved his hand over her nose. At this point, she relented and buried her head into his armpit, releasing all the tension from her body. After he placed the rope around her neck and improvised a halter, he went about trying to take the saddle off. While all this was going on, Chico fed quietly on some nearby plants as if nothing had happened. The saddle readjusted and secured in place, Bert mounted Chico and took off for Lake Louise leading Annabelle. Chico was stepping out like a colt again, satisfied everything had turned out well.

The next day, a pack string arrived from Temple, and Donny found out, to his great relief, that Annabelle had been found. Meanwhile, Ray's pack trip was nearly over, so Donny rushed off to meet up with the group. When he caught up to them later that day, the "moccasin telegraph" had already reached them.

"Yeth Donny, you're pretty good with people, and you can shoe a horthe well, but your father's a much better horthe-turd detective than you are," Ray said to Donny as he rode into camp.

CHAPTER

5

Donny and Keith's Horse Trip

KEITH FOSTER HAD A GREAT aversion to the taste of beans. He had no fondness for them as a kid in Millarville, but when he went to work for Bert Mickle in Lake Louise, he grew to hate them. Donny Mickle tolerated them more than Keith, but then he would eat almost anything. If he was hungry, he just opened the fridge and grabbed whatever was closest on the shelf. Although Donny thought ketchup could turn anything into haute cuisine, even beans took their toll after a while.

The Mickles seemed to have an abundance of beans, and they showed up without fail in the pack boxes on every horse trip. We would complain like a broken record to Bert and June, but those beans would always turn up among the other canned goods that were so popular in the can-happy 1960s. Beans extended a pot of stew for up to a week on the trail. After the second day, Bert would add a few cans of beans to the pot each additional night. This increased the volume, but also changed the ratio of meat to vegetables. To give the stew some colour and zip, he often added a can or two of Mexican-style corn. My abiding memory of Bert is of him leaning over a fire, stirring another can of something into the pot, a cigarette dangling from his lips.

In 1965, the year before I started to work for the Mickle outfit, Donny and Keith made a long trip from their hunting area in the Blackstone, north of Nordegg, Alberta, to the country just south of the Ya Ha Tinda Ranch. They had been assigned the chore of trailing the horses back to their wintering grounds. The two wranglers were looking forward to the trip, as they would be riding through country they hadn't seen in a while.

Now, Keith resembled a cartoon caricature; he had no chin and one eye that often watered. A silk neckerchief worn proudly around his skinny neck added colour to this simple picture. The neckerchief, as well as the rest of his western attire, would eventually become a signature of his style.

It was mid-October, and the region was enjoying one of those cherished spells of Indian summer. The days were blessed with deep blue skies, while warm winds caressed the land in the evenings. This is often the best time to be out on a trip in the montane grasslands of the frontal range.

Donny and Keith's Horse Trip

You know winter is just around the corner, and the threat of snow makes the season all the more special.

Faye and the last of the season's clients joined the cowboys on the long haul to the road. It was then Faye's job to repack the boxes for Donny and Keith's trip back to the wintering ground south of the Ya Ha Tinda. Like lazy slugs used to a routine, Donny and Keith lingered around the fire while Faye packed up provisions for them. She wondered why she couldn't be trailing the horses instead of Keith or Donny, but they ignored her complaints that this was an unjust world. Keith only inflamed the situation by boorishly offering his opinions on the role of women and suggesting that Faye should shut up and accept it. Keith would rue that moment later and wonder why he hadn't anticipated her revenge.

They were off early the next morning and were surprised when Faye handed them each a lunch. This was an unusual gesture on Faye's part, and it baffled Donny. Keith accepted it with no further thought. It would be their only meal on the long, 45-kilometre ride that first day.

Donny took the lead, leaving Keith to bring up the rear as they headed west for the Kootenay Plains. They were in good spirits as they rode along the gravel road. Between the riders were 18 head of horses, including two pack horses carrying their food and camp gear. Keith was always hungry and wondered what treat might be in store for him at supper that night. He hoped for some leftover meatloaf from the previous night's dinner. He loved meatloaf, and what's more, they wouldn't even need to heat it up. With that thought in mind, he pulled out his lunch and looked at the skimpy sandwich. He saw some mustard that seemed to announce the presence of some meat, so he bit into it with great anticipation.

"God damn it, Mickle!" Keith bellowed. "That miserable woman. I'm going to kill your sister!" With that, Donny was brought up to date on the state of Keith's sandwich. Faye had diligently laid two slices of waxed paper between two pieces of stale bread, like processed cheese. Spread over the paper was an adequate amount of mustard. In one corner lay the imprint of Keith's false teeth. Disgusted, he tossed the sandwich into the bush. Donny's sandwiches were only marginally better: two slices of bread with mustard, ketchup and nothing else. But to Donny, this was no hardship.

It wasn't until they approached the Kootenay Plains, where they would camp for the first night, that Keith's spirits improved. They camped down by the river in a grove of aspen and enjoyed an unobstructed view of the mountains to the west. It had been a hot summer so there wasn't even a hint of white on the distant mountains.

Keith was hungry, and before long he dived into the pack boxes, removing layers of jackets and pants until he finally reached the food at the bottom of the boxes. All he found were tins of beans. Two rows of damn beans. He let out a scream that got Donny's immediate and alarmed attention. Donny started into the second set of boxes, only to find pots and pans and kitchen utensils, but no food. Keith's eyes darted around the scattered camp. He began kicking things and cursing Faye. All Donny could do was watch. As close as he and Faye were, there was no love lost between them at moments like this.

They had enough beans to last at least a week or so, but that was small comfort when the only accompaniment was half a loaf of bread and a jar of sandwich spread. Simmering with resentment, they unrolled their bedrolls on the ground and threw the tent over them like a quilt. They built a fire and made sandwiches using the sandwich spread. Not the most appetizing meal, but better than canned beans.

The sound of horse bells awoke them the next morning. Donny got up first and lit a small fire. Neither spoke a word as they dressed, grabbed their halters and set off to retrieve the horses. It was comforting to find them nearby. After a breakfast of cold beans on the little bread that was left, they were off for the White Rabbit Valley.

Keith knew the country well and stationed himself in the lead, while Donny took up the rear, pushing the stragglers along. For the whole day, they saw little of each other as the horses spaced themselves out and settled into a reasonable pecking order. The wranglers had had a barely palatable breakfast and no lunch, so they looked forward to their arrival at the Indianhead warden station. Here, they hoped to run into the resident warden and a welcoming evening meal. First, though, they had to ascend the pass at the head of the White Rabbit River and climb the upper reaches of the Ram River. From there, it was over another pass to Indianhead Creek and Banff National Park.

Indianhead warden station is an unusual place. It sits in an open field of poplar and spruce, surrounded by a white pole fence, miles from any road. A bungalow in the middle of the wilderness strikes the unwary traveller as odd, yet intriguing and welcoming at the same time. Donny and Keith had been there before and had always been greeted by friendly and hospitable wardens. They envisioned the same that day and hoped to be fed a hearty meal and invited to stay for the night.

It was dusk when the pair pushed their 18 head of horses into the pasture near the station. They could see the warden's horses jumping around a small corral with their bells and hobbles on. They were met on the doorstep by Jim Rimmer. Jim was an eccentric Englishman who had recently joined the warden service and already had a reputation as being less than hospitable. The fact that it was almost dark didn't improve his disposition.

He interrogated Donny and Keith for a few minutes. Who were they? Where were they going? What were they up to? They told him that they worked for Bert Mickle and were heading for their winter range on the Red Deer River with 18 head of horses. Jim took this in and replied in his English accent, "Well, you boys look a little hungry. Perhaps I can rustle you up a spud." On hearing what sounded like

Indianhead warden cabin, Banff National Park.

a novel term for supper, they went in and sat down at the table, keeping up a lively conversation about the fortuitous Indian summer they were having.

Meanwhile, Jim took a potato, a fairly small one, and cut it into little slices. He put it in a frying pan, cooked it up and served it to the two hopeful cowboys on large plastic plates. The wilted pieces swam forlornly on the oversized plates, as though looking for a long-departed piece of meat. The boys looked up at each other and nearly giggled in disbelief. The meagre offering was a whole lot better than nothing, but it didn't stop the growling in their bellies. Optimism prevailed, however. They fully expected to be invited to stay the night and be offered a substantial breakfast befitting weary travellers. But Jim lived up to his reputation as an oddball loner. As if on cue, he looked at his watch and said, "You boys better get going; it's getting past my bedtime."

It was now pitch-dark. They bid a forlorn goodbye and headed out into the surrounding night. They both stayed in the rear of the herd, as they couldn't see where they were going. They knew some of the horses had been this way before, and their strategy was to follow rather than try to lead. White Lady, the infamous lead mare, was in the herd, and Donny and Keith tried to focus on her. Once in a while, they could make out her form in the gloom.

It was 12 kilometres to Harrison Flats, and they hoped the horses would lead them there. All they could do now was keep their heads down, hang on to their saddle horns and weave their way down the trail in this fashion. Once they reached the river, the horses were held to its course, as high clay banks hemmed them in. They followed down through the gravel beds, splashing across the river several times. Doubt about their route crept in, but the pair fought it off, hoping that the horses knew where they were going.

Eventually, they broke away from the river onto flat ground, and the horses stopped to feed. They unpacked the two pack horses and unsaddled and turned the horses loose with hobbles and bells for a well-deserved rest. The boys were now too tired to eat or even put up the tent. They rolled out their bedrolls on the ground, covered them with the tent, crawled in and went to sleep.

Now, a cowboy's bedroll is personal, well put together and well thought out. In those days, it was usually a big Artic 5 Star sleeping bag on top of an air mattress, all of it covered and surrounded by a canvas pack tarp. Inside the sleeping bag, an inner flannel sheet and a small pillow were squirrelled away. The whole thing was rolled up like a cabbage roll and secured with a tightly tied rope. That way it was easy to lay out. All you did was untie the knot and roll it out.

Donny and Keith woke up in the morning with a downy quilt of snow 30 centimetres thick on top of their sleeping bags. It was a harsh world they now faced as they crawled out from under the blanket of snow. Some of their kitchen gear had been scattered about the night before, and they went around kicking in the snow here and there, looking for their equipment. There was little thought of making breakfast, even though they hadn't eaten anything of substance for a couple of days. Only beans remained, and that didn't inspire them.

They heard some bells and in good time managed to catch two saddle horses and the pack horses. They led them back to camp and packed up with numb fingers, stiff tarps and frozen lash ropes. At last, they gathered up the horses and headed for the Ya Ha Tinda Ranch, Depressed, cold and starving, the two forlorn figures hunkered down in their wet saddles. It was easy riding down the flats for several kilometres until they crossed the river to the south and headed into the trees. From here, it was another 24 kilometres to the ranch.

By midday, the sun had come out, and the snow on the ground started to melt. Steam rose from the backs of the horses, and the cowboys relished the heat. They were on a road that they had picked up near Forbidden Creek, and they pushed the horses into a trot. They made good time until they neared the ranch buildings of the Ya Ha Tinda.

Here, all of a sudden, the horses stampeded. These horses had seen almost everything in a wilderness setting and grazed with moose, elk and grizzly bears, but they had never seen a milk cow with a big bell around her neck. With their tails held high and to the accompaniment of snappy farts, the herd took off en masse like rifle shots. Donny and Keith rode hard to get ahead of them and slow them down. It only seemed to take minutes to cover the ground from the ranch buildings to the Big Horn campsite on the Red Deer River, a distance of three or four kilometres. It was here that Bert was supposed to meet them with fresh food.

When they got there, there was no sign of him. The horses had calmed down, so they turned them loose. It was almost dark, and they argued about whether they should set up the tent or not.

"We don't need the tent up," Donny said. "We haven't used it yet on the trip."

"We're suppose to sleep inside it, not under it," Keith retorted. "It did snow last night you know, or did you miss that?" Keith's sarcasm prevailed, and they set up the tent. It was no easy chore, as it was an old canvas wall tent that needed wooden poles and pegs. When it was all done, they sat around a big roaring fire and cursed Bert for not being there with fresh food.

In a foul mood aggravated by hunger, they argued about whether to eat canned beans or hold out for Bert's arrival in the morning. That, however, was probably too optimistic. It was then that their tortured minds came up with an effective way to make sure that they would never see the beans again. They put the cans of beans in the fire and watched them roast.

The flames licked around the cans' paper labels. The boys were getting a little bushed by now, but they were still rational enough to step away from the fire and watch from behind some trees. The cans swelled like bloated ticks on the back of a moose. Suddenly, there was a huge roar, like dynamite exploding. The cans burst so violently that they blew the fire out. Donny and Keith looked at the remains of the fire, then at each other, and rolled on the ground, clutching their stomachs and laughing like hyenas. There were beans hanging on everything: trees, tents, tack and themselves. Beans clung to their shirts and faces. It was the greatest joke they had ever pulled off. When they saw their tent, peppered and splattered in brown beans, they howled again, almost choking in their mirth. They ended the evening with an improvised chicken dance around the fire as the last remnants of the coals glowed in the night.

The following morning, Donny woke up with the ridge-pole just about touching his nose, bent low under the weight of fresh snow—a good foot of it. Donny was not amused that it was always him who had to get up and build a fire, even though his bladder got him up first in the morning. As he crawled out of his bedroll, Keith said smugly, "See, I told you we needed to put the tent up, Mickle."

"Yeah, yeah. You're finally right for a change."

Keith suggested they go up to the ranch house and beg for some food, but Donny quashed that idea. He wasn't quite that desperate, although he finally succumbed to hunger and managed what remained of the beans for brunch. Keith flatly refused. They were pretty testy with each other by now; it had been a tough trip and a long hunting season, and all they both wanted was to have a hot shower somewhere and get some decent restaurant food. They thought about trying to catch a fish in the river, but kept putting it off. Around four o'clock, Bert's arrival broke the tedium.

They ranted and raged and gave Bert heck, as Keith, in particular, applied his sharp, switchblade tongue. When Bert saw the brown stuff hanging from the trees and all over his tent, he gladly feigned distraction from the verbal abuse and became inquisitive. All Keith said as he climbed into the truck was, "Don't ever feed us damn beans again." They told Bert he had to buy them the biggest steak in Sundre and off they drove. It was two hours to Sundre on a dirt and gravel road, and when they got there, as luck would have it, the restaurant was closed. They went to the bar in the hotel and started drinking beer. The only things you could get to eat in a bar back then were potato chips, peanuts, pickled eggs, pepperoni or Piggy Puffs.

Though it was the end of the trip, it was not the end of their association with Jim Rimmer. They both ran into Jim a year later in the Mount Royal Hotel in Banff. They certainly didn't offer to buy him a beer and only said a curt hello as they sat down some distance away.

Jim fell into the Clearwater River the following winter on his way to Indianhead warden station. He was on snow-shoes, patrolling the district far from the station. It was -40°C, and by the time he got to the station, he had severe frostbite. He lost all of his toes and parts of both feet, but it didn't stop him being a park warden. The only thing he ever complained about was that the toes of his riding boots always seemed to curl up.

CHAPTER

6

Stuck in the Muck

I AWOKE ONE MORNING TO THE sound of prowlers outside the cabin at the Yoho National Park horse ranch. I could hear movement and the rustle of tall grass, then a muffled voice. Someone laughed—it was more like a cackle—and said, "The son-of-a-bitch is around here somewhere." A figure passed by the far window, wearing a cowboy hat and a plaid wool jacket. He stopped and peered in with his hand shading his eyes. It was Bert Mickle, and he was cackling again. Then I heard Donny say, "Come on, Portman, open the door, we want some coffee." They were up to no good.

It was Donny's turn to feed the horses that day, and he was an early riser. Bert was visiting and came along to say hello and to see if he could catch me unawares in bed. I made some coffee and started getting ready for work. They took the hint, drained their cups and went off to feed the horses. It was eight o'clock.

The sun illuminated the meadow and lingered on the backs of the horses grazing quietly on new grass. I felt inspired. It would be a fine day to take the colt out. Every year the Ya Ha Tinda ranch boss sends out young colts to learn the real work from one of the more horse-wise wardens in the mountain parks, and this year I was breaking in Lane. He was a tall and spindly black gelding who needed a lot of work because he was skittish and spooked easily at anything unfamiliar.

I also thought it would be a chance to go riding with Kathy Calvert, Canada's first female park warden, and assess her skill with horses. She said she had grown up with them, but that was a while ago, and people often overestimated their abilities when applying for the job. You certainly can't tell from an interview what an individual is capable of. Over the years I have come to believe it is often a patient and quiet personality that makes for success with horses, rather than a lot of experience.

When Kathy and I returned from the warden office, Bert and Donny were gone. I saddled her up with Red, a reliable, stout gelding that had a great temperament and was the favourite of everyone in the park. I watched her carefully as she groomed and saddled Red without any sign of nervousness and was reassured when she mounted easily. I wish I had had the same success. Lane was on eggshells that day, and it took patience to get saddled and mounted without a bucking spree. The first obstacle of the day was getting across the Trans-Canada Highway. This was one of the drawbacks of the ranch location. All the easily accessible trails were on the north side of the highway, and there was no choice but to head in that direction. I reasoned that this would be good experience for Lane, and there was no time like the present to get him used to the unfamiliar sights and sounds.

We crossed the highway without mishap. Kathy was obviously relishing the ride, and soon we were out on the open Kicking Horse River flats—a stunning area rarely seen by the public. The river runs through a variety of terrain, and Lane had plenty to get used to. Red's calm approach to everything around him set the example. I decided to make it a fairly long day to work on Lane's conditioning and give him a chance to really settle down.

We stopped for lunch at a pleasant little pool and lay back to enjoy the first warm day of spring. Over sandwiches, Kathy and I talked as we watched the horses graze avidly on the lush green grass. I was feeling refreshed and confident at how the ride was going and decided we would do a little exploring on some high benches on the south side of the highway before heading home.

Again, there was no problem getting across the Trans-Canada, and soon we were working our way through a dense, north-facing coniferous forest that required some negotiating. Everything came at us: small meandering streams with undercut banks, a young white-tailed deer springing away in alarm and lots of dead trees and thick willow. At times, I let Kathy take the lead, especially when we had to jump deadfall or squeeze through thick timber. Red was a pro, and since Kathy hadn't ridden in a mountain environment before, it was good for her to learn what horses could and could not handle.

It was all good experience, but soon I figured enough was enough. The bush bashing was getting tedious, and it was time to go home. With this in mind, I decided to take a shorter route than the one Kathy was taking. I rode ahead to what appeared to be an open meadow to get some relief from the bush, which was becoming oppressive. The afternoon sun slanted across the opening, making the air hazy as it shone through the dust rising off old cattails. The cattails should have been the clue, but I was puzzled by the odd appearance of the meadow. It was a grey green colour, but certainly looked solid enough.

In the middle of the meadow was a large patch of perfectly flat ground. On closer inspection, it looked like a dry mud flat, all cracked and fissured. What I didn't know was that there was a layer of water a few centimetres deep on top. It was clear and still as glass. If I'd known this, I would not have ventured closer.

Lane blundered on in this totally unfamiliar environment, until the ground unexpectedly gave way and I realized

Trailing horses near the Panther River.

we were on the edge of a swamp. The inexperienced colt from the hard plains of Alberta had never come across ground like this. With little warning, he bolted forward, thinking he might just run through it, and suddenly we were well out in the middle and sinking fast.

I was just able to yell to Kathy to stay away from the swamp, but Red was too bush-wise to get into the same trouble. She looked on helplessly as I bailed off and promptly started sinking myself. Lane groaned and slipped sideways,

96

making it difficult for him to get his feet under him. The slippery clay and mud on the slough bottom held Lane's legs with ever-tightening suction, and he thrashed about pathetically trying to get his legs underneath him, but to no avail. I knew things were serious when he gave up struggling and continued to sink, now nearly completely on his side. I was up past my knees, but had hit the clay bottom and could move somewhat.

As soon as she saw our predicament, Kathy secured her horse and waded out to help. She is not very tall, and by the time she reached Lane, the water was up around her thighs. There was little to do but keep Lane's head up and try and get help for him.

I figured if we could get some poles under Lane we could prop him up until he could get out under his own steam. I left Kathy holding his head clear of the water, while I waded out of the swamp and went to find what I could in the bush. There was plenty of dead wood around, and I soon returned with a few stout logs, which we jammed under the tired horse to try and lever him upright. We exhausted ourselves with this effort, but it was futile. I realized then that the only way to save him was to drag him out with more horses and ropes. This meant one of us would have to go for help.

Since I was familiar with the country, we decided it was best if I went back to the highway to guide a rescue crew in. There was no way anyone would find us in the thick bush without help. Luckily, the radio was dry and safe in Kathy's saddlebag. I radioed out to the warden office, requesting whoever was available to load a couple of horses and head out toward Ottertail, close to where we were riding. I added, "Bring lots of rope and a gun." If we couldn't save Lane from the water, we could at least save him from an agonizingly slow death.

If Kathy heard this, she didn't say anything, but by now I realized that she would have come to the same conclusion herself. She grimaced at me as she continued to support Lane's head, saying only that I should hurry or she might sink out of sight.

I rode quickly on staunch old Red to meet Randy Robertson, who had responded to the call. He had brought Elva, a solid young mare, considerable rope and the requested rifle. Despite moving with all dispatch, it was still nearly an hour before we got back to Kathy. Lane lay with his back facing the shore. Up to her armpits in the mud, Kathy was still stoically holding up his head, but her relief was evident. She had to be thoroughly chilled by now.

We found more poles for leverage and ran the rope out to Lane. His saddle was still in place, which provided plenty of purchase for the rope. Once the rope was rigged, Kathy remained with Lane, beating on his rump, while Randy and I drove the two pulling horses. They repeatedly gave a mighty effort, but simply could not budge him. I left Randy on shore and went to help Kathy with the poles.

Once again, both horses pulled as we tried to force Lane

to his feet. He tried valiantly to stand up and get his feet under him, but the mud held him fast on his side like an insect on flypaper. If we were to get Lane out, he would have to give us all the help he could, but he was exhausted and demoralized with the effort. We tried again, and this time poor Elva foundered on the shore. We stopped then to give everyone a break. I was getting more and more desperate, truly afraid I would have to use the rifle.

Lane began to struggle again. Slowly, his angle started to improve, getting more and more in line with the shore. Finally, he got one leg under his chest. We got the pulling horses back in position. At that point, Red looked back. To this day, I believe I detected a look of pity—and then of resolve. He momentarily nuzzled Elva, then both heaved mightily on the ropes while we pushed and beat on Lane. He thrust forward with a huge effort, and suddenly he was free, up and lunging toward the shore. I thought he would never stop. He bolted out of the swamp as though it were on fire. If he hadn't been held by the rope, he probably would have run all the way to the northern confines of the park.

Randy laughed as Kathy fell back in the swamp, worn out by the effort. We watched Lane as he trembled and then exhaled deeply through his nose. With a nervous energy, he started to feed on the tender grasses, as if he were trying to put the awful experience behind him. The rope was coiled and the rifle packed away before we rode quietly back to the ranch.

I have never forgotten the feeling of empathy the rescue horses seemed to have for Lane. He was just a colt, and they knew he was close to losing his life. Although we had done everything we could for the horse, in the end, it was the valiant efforts of Elva and Red that saved him.

7

The Swinging Bridge

IN 1986, A COUPLE OF good friends, Art Twomey and Margie Jamieson, decided to undertake an ambitious pack trip along the Continental Divide with some mules and a saddle horse each. They set out from Canal Flats, BC, and planned to use the summer months to make it as far as Mt. Sir Alexander, a remote and fascinating area north of Mt. Robson. It was a three-month journey that would take them through some of the most spectacular country Banff and Jasper national parks had to offer.

Part of their journey led them east of the Icefield Parkway (the Banff–Jasper Highway) into the remote Siffleur Wilderness. En route, they restocked in Banff, then headed north across the Red Deer River and up the

Clearwater River to a nice campsite below Devon Lakes. Kathy and I, who were married by that time, had previously arranged to meet Art and Margie here with a couple of pack horses loaded with fresh supplies. We set out from Lake Louise up the Pipestone, intending to get to Devon Lakes over the Pipestone and Clearwater passes. On the way up the Pipestone, we ran across a couple of young Swiss men leading two horses that had riding saddles on them. Two large packs hung from the saddle horns. The packs were rearranged onto one animal whenever they encountered a river crossing. One of the men would ride across leading the pack-laden animal, dump the packs on the far shore and then come back with the horses to pick up the second man. They negotiated some substantial river crossings this way without getting wet.

These boys were living their dream of travelling through the Canadian Rockies on horseback. They had bought two broken-down sorrels from a less than honest farmer around Calgary and had somehow made it from Banff to Lake Louise knowing very little about horses. They intended to travel all the way to Jasper, more or less via the same route as Art and Margie. When we met them, they had already been informed by the Banff warden service that the horses could not be tied up all night, as they needed to graze and recoup their energy.

When I asked them how they were managing with the horses, they gave me a rather puzzled look, shrugged their shoulders and said they were getting by. I gathered from their broken English that at night they would turn one horse loose to graze while the other remained tied up. At about midnight they would switch the animals and, in that fashion, the horses were fed and remained in close proximity to their camp.

We left them and continued our journey north and east to meet Art and Margie at Devon Lakes. Besides fresh food, we also had the camping permits they needed to get through Jasper National Park.

The campsite below Devon Lakes is one of the most tranquil and peaceful spots around. Well suited for horses, it is located at the edge of a dark spruce forest next to a lush meadow, with open, level ground and a convenient brook that gurgles cheerfully nearby. Art and Margie were in camp and well rested when we arrived, as they had got there the previous day. They had their teepee up and a small fire going. They greeted us warmly and helped us unload the pack horses. Soon we were settled down by the fire, while the horses grazed nearby. They filled us in on their trip, and Art showed us several pan-sized trout he had caught at Devon Lakes. He prepared them with herbs and spices, wrapping each individually in tin foil. They were soon sizzling away in the open fire.

Kathy and I had brought some fiddlehead greens and rice, plus a bottle of white wine that complemented the fish nicely. Afterwards, we relaxed around the fire telling stories and catching up on each other's lives. We took notice of the two Swiss men, who showed up at dusk, still leading their horses. They camped a good distance away from us, seeming to want their privacy, which suited us fine.

We spent the next day in a leisurely fashion, exploring the surrounding area and catching a few more fish. They added greatly to the wholesome breakfast we prepared the following morning before breaking camp. We intended to travel another day with Art and Margie before leaving them to their northern journey. The ride to the pass and over to the Siffleur River was spectacular under deep blue skies that silhouetted the jagged peaks. As we travelled down the Siffleur Valley, snaking across the river in many places, we felt we had the land all to ourselves. We had left the Swiss behind, as they were having an extra layover day, allowing the two parties to gain some distance between each other.

We got to Isabella Lake early that afternoon, foregoing camp in lieu of a pleasant warden's cabin. That evening, Art and I, wearing shorts and running shoes, waded across a deep channel to the other side of Isabella Lake. Rainbow trout often lurked on a shallow shelf on this side.

The lake can be difficult to fish in the first half of the summer, when it clouds over with silt washed down from the melting glaciers. The silt creates the opaque turquoise colour seen in many mountain lakes at that time of year. Later in the summer, it clears to a deep crystal blue shade, making for great fishing. The water was cool, but we soon forgot about that as we concentrated on fishing for trout.

Isabella Lake, Banff National Park.

On this particular evening, the water was as smooth as glass right across the lake. The trout began to rise and feed on the surface insects just as we arrived. Art had his fly rod out and assembled in a matter of minutes and soon had a splashing rainbow near at hand, slapping water all over his torso and face. The big trout put on a real display. Art played it for a while before expertly coaxing the fish into the landing net.

It took a little longer for me to get my collapsible rod

together and my reel in place, but soon I had my spinner on—a red and white, size eight Len Thompson. The shelf was six or seven metres away, and I cast diagonally across it and well beyond, working back slowly, just enough to give the spoon adequate action. As the lure crossed the line of dark vegetation that marked the shelf, there was a sudden hit on the line. A substantial amount of wiggling resonated up the rod. I played the fish for quite some time, then started to reel it in.

We fished like this until we had caught two each. The sound of our splashing, laughter and light banter carried easily on the smooth surface of the lake. The girls could hear us plainly a kilometre away as they sat and read in the angled beam of the evening sun. Behind them, the cabin had taken on a rich and oily texture. Illuminated by the slanting sunlight, it flashed continually across the lake like a beacon. When the sun went behind the mountain and dusk settled over the landscape, we returned to the cabin, shivering, cold and ready for a hearty fish dinner.

Kathy and I said goodbye to Art and Margie the next morning. They were continuing their journey north down the Siffleur River to where it finally enters the North Saskatchewan River at the Kootenay Plains. We were heading over Dolomite Pass to the trailhead at Crowfoot Lookout, near Bow Lake on the Icefield Parkway.

Our trip out was uneventful, broken only by the welcome transition from rock-strewn fields to the expanse of alpine meadows and blue lakes scooped out by long-receded glaciers. After we broke through a crack in the rock at the top of Dolomite Pass, we caught sight of the highway in the distance. Helen Lake, far below, oval and serene with its velvet green shoulders, urged us on.

Art and Margie continued down through the deep forest of the mid-Siffleur until they reached Bert Mickle's old hunting camp. From here, they followed an old seismic line that eventually deposited them amidst the green grass and aspen stands that make up much of the Kootenay Plains periphery. When they hit the North Saskatchewan River, they were taken aback by its size and colour. It no longer carried the silt of melting glaciers and was cleaner and much bluer.

The North Saskatchewan is not an easy river to cross in August, as it is wide, swift and deep. Entering and exiting is straightforward, as there are no sharp drops along its bank in this section. However, once in the water, the horses are committed to swimming almost the whole width of the river. It seems forever before their feet start to hit bottom again. Some never learn how to swim properly, and others have so little buoyancy that they almost walk along the bottom.

The Swiss pair had taken the same route and soon met up with Art and Margie again. The river is notoriously tough to cross, and both Art and Margie were worried about how the two men—boys really—would manage with their dubious horses.

There is a long, swinging suspension bridge for foot traffic, just wide enough for hikers, right at the river crossing. The bridge is made of spaced wooden planks, with gaps just wide enough to fit a wayward foot. Our friends carried all their boxes and duffel across the bridge—time-consuming and hard work, but it allowed the mules to swim the river safely, unencumbered with heavy packs. Margie had never crossed such a large river with her mare before and decided to swim the river with her and the mules.

Just as they got into the current, Margie realized her horse couldn't swim. Before she could react, Margie was upside down and sinking fast beneath her saddle horse. When a horse is having trouble swimming, it's usually best to get off and catch the horse's tail if possible. This way the horse will pull you across to the far shore. But Margie had no horse to hang on to. She got back to the near shore just in time to see the mare float down the river under the bridge. To her relief, the horse washed up on the same side as she did, a considerable distance downstream from where they started. The mules were better at this endeavour and crossed with ease, emerging eventually on the other side. Art was there to meet them, but was now concerned for Margie and her horse. How would they ever entice the horse back into the river and get her to the far shore?

The two boys had arrived just in time to see the spectacle and had no intention of repeating it. They had seen the size of the river and the swinging bridge, and watched as horse and rider foundered in the rushing water. After considering their options, they decided to walk their two horses across the slatted bridge. To Art's astonishment, the horses complacently negotiated the swaying, bouncing bridge as though they were veterans of a three-ring circus act.

Margie's horse, now thoroughly alarmed at the prospect of having to swim again, saw this solution and decided it was the only way to go. Before they knew it, the mare joined the other two and nimbly crossed the bridge behind them. The boys and the three horses all arrived safe and sound on the other side. A wet and bedraggled Margie soon joined them.

This is not the recommended way to get your horses across the river at Kootenay Plains. In fact, it would be almost impossible to get a horse to repeat the stunt suspended high above the North Saskatchewan River. For the Swiss, ignorance was bliss, and for Art and Margie, it would be one of many memorable highlights of a remarkable trip along the Continental Divide.

CHAPTER

8

The Eccentric
Jim Rimmer

PERRY JACOBSON GREW UP IMMERSED in ranching life. His parents originally had a spread near Medicine Hat, Alberta. Then, when he was 16, they moved to the Millarville area. They bought the old Millar place, a famous ranch established between 1883 and 1885, and many of the original buildings were still standing. As a youth, Perry was into rodeo and spent much of his free time going to different events as a roper. In the fall, the family would set out for the nearby mountains with their pack horses to do some hunting.

Although Perry had a strong background with horses and rodeo, he was also a good student and went on to university. His real passion, however, was for the outdoors and doing what he loved best—riding horses. So it was no surprise that he was attracted to the warden service and got hired on. Perry became a seasonal warden in 1972 in Banff National Park—part of a new wave of young wardens with a post-secondary education. One of Perry's early assignments was to help out Jim Rimmer, who was stationed at Saskatchewan River Crossing. Jim, by contrast, was an "old school" warden and very set in his ways.

That summer, Jim had no seasonal warden assigned to help him out. Every time he came to Lake Louise, he would complain to his boss that he was getting no help. On one particular occasion, he wanted to go up the Howse River and collect the winter's supply of firewood. Perry was the low man on the totem pole at that time, so was selected to go.

Jim's reputation preceded him. Larry Gilmar, Perry's boss, had already regaled Perry with many stories about the eccentric Englishman. Perry didn't mind going. He was looking forward to meeting Jim and getting to know him better. As Perry was preparing to depart, Larry suddenly blurted out—like a long-overdue confession—that if it got too rough out there, he should just come home.

Jim was in a bad mood when the two met. After brief introductions, they went down to the corral to get the horses ready. Perry was looking forward to getting out and away from the office. He had no idea what his role would be, but he thought that with his horse experience he would be on more or less equal terms with Jim. Perry went to catch his horse.

"No, no, no, you can't do that," Jim commanded. "You just watch me."

"I'm quite comfortable with horses. I was raised on a ranch," said Perry.

"Well, well," Jim said in his English accent, "we'll see about that." Perry didn't want to cause any trouble, so he sat back and watched.

Jim strolled into the corral among the horses. A lariat twirled around his head like a ground-tied helicopter desperately trying to lift off. The horses stampeded counterclockwise around him in a cloud of dust, hugging the inside of the rail fence. The faster he twirled the rope, the harder they ran. After rousing the horses to a frenzy, Jim put the rope aside and waited in the swirling clouds of dust for the horses to settle down. It took a long time, but finally they all came to a stop, their backs up against the fence and their eyes bulging with alarm as they eyed Jim in the centre of the corral. Perry quietly caught his horse and, without a word, left the corral to Jim and his unusual antics. Eventually, the horses were saddled, and then it was time to pack the boxes with their food and duffel.

"Did you bring your food?"

"Yeah," said Perry. "I went and bought supplies through the government."

"Huh," Jim said, "I don't do that. I go on my own rations."

Perry offered to help pack up the horses, but Jim would have nothing to do with that. He instructed Perry to stand back while he made sure they were packed to his liking. Now, the diamond made by the lash ropes on a pack horse is supposed to be positioned on the top and in the middle of the pack, but because Jim was trying too hard to get a tight diamond, he pulled it well over to one side. Perry decided to let it be and not say anything, as Jim seemed so touchy about accepting any help and also appeared to have little regard for Perry's capabilities.

Perry watched as Jim tailed the pack horses in a string. Perry offered to lead a pack horse, making it easier for Jim, but the man wanted nothing to do with that notion, either. Jim tied the halter shank of one pack horse to the tail of another, but unwittingly left the rope between them too long. There was two metres of slack, and Perry pointed this out to Jim.

"My ponies are all right, you'll see," was all he said. And with that they headed out, followed closely by Jim's dog, Spook, a white English bull terrier.

They arrived at the Mistaya River. The water was high after the recent rains and laden with big boulders that rolled along the bottom and made for a treacherous crossing. It was "bobbing water," which meant the water level was well past the horses' bellies.

Jim barged into the river leading the pack horses, giving them little chance to anticipate how they were going to negotiate the crossing. Spook jumped in upstream of the horses, and was immediately swept away by the current. Despite his panicky dog-paddling, he was being carried down toward the horses. He was struggling madly just above the last pack horse before he was swept up against it, then disappeared under the horse's belly, only to pop up on the other side. Away he went, bobbing on the waves like a sailor, as Jim yelled, "Swim for it, Spook, swim for it." Spook was swept all the way down to where the Mistaya runs into the North Saskatchewan River—almost a kilometre. He came out on the far shore, but he just about drowned. When he caught up to the rest of the group, the dog took off like a shot. Jim spent the rest of the day yelling, "Here, Spook. Where are you, Spook?" but the dog was long gone.

In the meantime, the pack horse that Spook had been swept under had come unglued, and when they reached the far shore, he jumped ahead and stepped right over the halter shank. Jim was oblivious to all this, thinking only of his dog receding from view. The horse hopped along trying to keep up, and Perry finally yelled at Jim to stop. Once he got Jim's attention, Perry stopped, climbed off his saddle horse and got the pack string straightened out. Around this time, the nearly drowned Spook finally showed up, much to Jim's relief.

They got up the trail about three kilometres when Bog, the last pack horse, stepped over the rope again. Bog pulled back immediately, stopping the pack horse ahead of him, whose tail was being yanked on with great gusto. This, in turn, halted the pack horse Jim was leading. Jim had fastened a loop at the end of the pack horse's halter shank and dropped it over his saddle horn. This is something you never do if you want to stay alive. The halter shank from the pack horse Jim was leading was now firmly secured to Jim's saddle, making it impossible to release when the horse pulled back. When this happened, Jim suddenly found himself and his saddle horse perpendicular to the pack string.

By now, Bog was in a state of real terror, pulling back and bucking as the pack on his back started to fall apart. With all the pack horses now pulling back madly, neither Jim nor Cindy, his saddle horse, had a chance. Down they went in a cloud of dust, as Perry gaped in horror at the unfolding wreck. When Cindy went down, the rope came off the saddle horn and the pack horses all flew backwards into a giant heap.

In the blink of an eye, Perry flicked his knife and cut the rope between the two pack horses and the still-standing Bog, who immediately took off, dragging ropes, pack tarps and boxes behind him. Perry managed to get the other two pack horses up on their feet and checked on Jim, who was stunned and dishevelled. Once he realized Jim was unhurt, Perry headed off to retrieve Bog and the scattered gear. If he wanted to survive the trip, Perry would have to watch Jim very closely from that moment on.

They finally got things sorted out, and Perry asked if he could lead Bog.

"You can lead him now." No argument there. When they got to Howse Cabin, Perry looked after the horses while Jim went inside to light the stove. Just before going in, Jim commented, "I noticed you're not too bad with horses. You can unsaddle them."

Perry stood by the hitching rail at the front of the cabin, happy with this new-found recognition. He could see Jim through the open doorway. There was an old four-lid stove in the cabin, and Jim was pouring white gas onto the logs as a starter for the fire. Perry watched this, thinking it was a terrible lot of white gas to be putting on the wood, when Jim struck the match. He threw the match in the stove, and suddenly there was a huge KABOOM! Flames engulfed Jim where he stood. All the lids blew out of the stove, levitating in mid-air for a split second, one lid carrying on up to hit the ceiling. It was a flat white ceiling, and the lid hit with a forceful "thwang," leaving a perfect black circle. Down they all came, crashing and clattering as Jim came out of the cabin slapping at his eyebrows. He turned around, pale with ash, the hair around his face totally singed, and said, "Tea will be ready in a minute."

They had come up the valley to get some wood, and that's what they put their minds to in the ensuing days. They went off into the bush and found a spot with plenty of dead standing timber, including a large spruce that was going to be a chore to skid to the cabin. Perry had worked in the logging industry as a faller for several years and asked Jim if he wanted him to fall the trees.

"No," Jim replied, "you just stand back and watch."

"I know how to fall trees," Perry said, but Jim told him just to observe.

Jim had tied old Barney about 15 metres from where he was cutting the big spruce. Perry noticed from the way Jim had notched the tree that it was going to fall on top of the horse. He went over to Jim and pointed this out.

"No, it's fine," Jim said abruptly. Perry was persistent, and Jim continued, "All right, move the old bastard if it's going to make you feel better." With that, Perry moved Barney. Sure as anything, after jamming the chainsaw a few times, Jim brought the old spruce down with a crash. It wiped out the entire area where the horse had been standing.

When the dust settled, Jim looked over at Perry and said, "It's a good thing we moved that horse."

The pair spent five days cutting wood, and every day brought another event. The trees were big, and they bucked them up into one- or two-metre lengths. Normally, you would skid logs using a horse, but Jim had other plans. He planned to pack the logs to the cabin on old Barney, one on each side of the horse. This was a huge load for the horse, but Perry's protests fell on deaf ears. When Jim made up his mind, nothing would change it.

They tried to pack thick logs, almost two metres long and half the diameter of a 45-gallon drum, on either side of the horse like two pack boxes. But because the logs were so heavy and unwieldly, both men needed to work on one side at a time. It was a tricky manoeuvre, because once one side was secure, it was imperative to tie up the other side before the weight of the first log pulled the saddle over. If not done quickly enough, the saddle would roll and all hell could break loose.

They were struggling with the weight of the second log when Barney started to jump around, forcing them to follow while trying to hold up the weight. As Perry recounted later, "We tried to roll this damn log on the side of the horse. It was at least five feet long and we were busting a gut trying to get this thing up there, when all of a sudden there was this huge fart." A branch on the log they were trying to load must have poked Barney in the ribs. The horse gave off a long, drawn-out fart that scared him as much as the logs did, and he was gone. The men were standing there, exasperated, watching Barney make good his escape, when Jim suddenly disappeared. One minute he was there, the next he was following the horse feet first with a basket rope looped around his foot.

Jim got acquainted with some serious bush, undergrowth and deadfall in his travels behind the horse. Perry tried to follow as best he could, but riding boots are not designed for sprinting. After a long time, the rope came unravelled from Jim's foot, and he came to rest in a heap at the base of a towering Engelmann spruce.

It took Perry about five minutes to catch Barney, about the time it took Jim to regain consciousness. Unbelievably, he hadn't broken anything. Jim moved very slowly and softly for a few days after that, but soon returned to his cranky old self.

During the time Jim convalesced, they continued to work at bringing in the wood. And as Perry said, "These wild events went on and on with frequent regularity." Jim went into a deep depression. He talked little and spent his quiet time alone reading a book, which suited Perry just fine.

The cabin was partitioned, separating the bedroom from the kitchen, which allowed the pair their own personal space: Perry had the kitchen and Jim the bedroom. They only shared the same room at night when they were asleep or when they ate a meal together. At times, Jim would go into a black mood and stop speaking altogether.

Jim used to suffer from bad asthma attacks. He had a little tube with a propeller on it that he used to suck on. Lying in bed on an army cot in the back room, Jim would suck on it so hard that Perry imagined he could almost hover. Before long, Perry noticed that the dog often slept on Jim's chest at night. Spook wasn't a big dog, but he was heavy, and this couldn't have helped Jim's asthma. The white dog rose and fell on Jim's chest in the moonlight, and every time Jim breathed in, a sort of whizzing sound came out of him, followed by the sound of air escaping a slowly deflating tire. It kept Perry awake for hours.

Another one of Jim's peculiarities was never hobbling his horses. "Don't these horses ever pull out?" Perry said one day. You always had to phrase things as a question with Jim if you expected to get a decent explanation and not have a fight on your hands.

"No, no," he said, "my ponies like me. They'll be here. Don't you worry."

Well, each day they were found farther and farther from the cabin. One morning, Jim left at 7:00 a.m. with a bridle in his hand and a small sack of oats to catch the horses. By 11:00 a.m. he hadn't returned, and Perry was concerned. Around noon, he heard a racket and saw the horses come careening around the corner. Perry scampered out and caught them and put them in the corral. Considering Jim's track record, Perry saddled his horse, figuring Jim might be in trouble.

Perry headed out on his saddle horse in the direction of the river. He met Jim not far from the cabin. He was wearing hip waders, the ones the pack rats had chewed holes in. Crossing the river in the awkward things, he had fallen in, filling them to the brim with water. He squished with every step, and small fountains squirted out through the holes.

They got back to the cabin, packed up and were soon on the trail again, heading for Saskatchewan River Crossing. By the time they got on the trail, Jim was happy. You could always tell when Jim was having a good day by the unusual tune he would sing, over and over again. Similar to the ring of a bell, a strong "d" was followed by an ever weakening "eee," then a few seconds later another "deee."

When they got to Saskatchewan River Crossing and

stepped off their horses, Jim was in a good mood. He looked over at Perry and said, "By God, we make a pretty good team." It had never occurred to Perry that they made a good team. "I'll get some photographs of the trip developed for you," Jim added.

"Yeah, I noticed you've been taking some pictures," said Perry.

"Yes, I document all my trips, you know."

Perry saw Jim about a month later and asked if he ever got his pictures back.

"What pictures?" Jim asked.

"Well, up the Howse River, of course."

"Oh, those," Jim said. "Hmm, I had the damn lens cap on the whole time. Didn't get any of the trip."

9

Trailing Horses
from the Ya Ha Tinda

ONE OF THE MORE THRILLING EVENTS of the year for many park wardens happens in the spring when the horses return from the Ya Ha Tinda for the summer's work. The event heralds the coming season and the long days full of excitement and adventure spent looking after a national park in the Canadian Rockies. In past years, the horses were brought back by truck, but that all changed when Banff National Park hired a new chief park warden who enjoyed riding and getting out in the backcountry. Gaby Fortin was from Quebec, and with typical French-Canadian passion, he embraced everything about horses and the western lifestyle.

Gaby reasoned it would be good to trail the horses back through the park once the passes were free of snow and the trails were open. It was a bonding exercise for the staff and helped settle the horses into the idea of going back to work again. Fresh off the range, the horses were full of vim and vigour. The long distance made for a gruelling trip for the first ride of the year, as muscles and backsides accustomed to soft truck seats over the winter took the brunt of the load.

Not just anyone was asked to go. Only those with experience were considered, and it was a privilege to be asked to participate. When Gaby Fortin decided to trail the horses, he felt it wouldn't be worthwhile unless the Kootenay and Yoho horses were included as well. Diplomatically, one person from each park was asked along. Usually, it was the barn boss or an experienced senior warden.

I was pleased when Gaby offhandedly asked if I'd be interested in going one spring. I had considerable experience with horses, having worked for Parks Canada in Jasper, Banff and Yoho national parks. Even though I had the background, it was nice to get the recognition and be singled out for the trip. I suppressed my excitement around the warden office, knowing I could let it all out when I got home to tell my wife. She would understand.

Kathy was a park warden working in Yoho National Park, just across the provincial border from Lake Louise, where we lived. It was a good arrangement. We didn't have to work in the same park, and the drive from Lake Louise to the boundary of Yoho was only eight kilometres. Kathy was a good rider and an experienced backcountry traveller.

I knew she would be happy for me and congratulate me for the opportunity it was.

She appeared to be as thrilled as I was. Of course, she wanted to know who was going from Yoho and was not surprised to hear it was Earl Hayes, the barn boss. Earl was an old hand with horses and had worked in Yoho for the past few years. He kept the string in good order and passed on his considerable experience and sound direction to all the new wardens in need of coaching. Kathy had worked closely with him in Yoho and had been given a young horse of her own to work with the previous year. It was worthy of her capabilities, and she was proud of her success with the filly. I tried not to gloat too much when I told her the details of the trip, but I saw the envy in her eyes.

A couple of days went by, and I got my gear in order. I downplayed the details with Kathy, sensing more envy each passing day. But one day Kathy came home looking like she had just won the lottery. In a sense, she had. She waltzed in, beaming gleefully. Unwittingly shattering my happiness, she announced, "You'll never guess what happened! Earl has to go to a wedding and can't make the trip. My boss said I could go instead!" She chattered away, not noticing my silent astonishment.

"No one else at work can handle that type of ride," she added. "Gord said there was no alternative, so I'm getting my stuff together tonight. It'll be great!"

I wasn't speechless for long. I stared at her as though she

was demented and uttered a string of oaths that I thought I'd left behind on the trail. How could she do this? I had the rare opportunity to go on a trip that was coveted by many in the warden service, a chance to be with the boys, chase horses across the country, drink whisky and tell tales into the wee hours.

And I had to take my wife!

It was insupportable! I sat down with a thud, wondering what had happened to my perfect world. How could I face the guys and tell them my wife was coming? Why couldn't I have married a teacher or a nurse?

I decided the best defence was offence. I derided her. I told her I wouldn't go if she was going. That was it. I wouldn't go and she would feel so bad that she would be forced to back out. Hell, they didn't need anyone from Yoho. They only had 13 horses anyway.

This tactic didn't get the results I wanted. She just said it was too bad I would miss such a good trip on her account, but Yoho must be represented and she was going and that was that. This really set me back: I didn't want to back out. My only choice now was to ignore her, pretend she didn't exist. The last thing I wanted was for the guys to think I had something to do with her going. That definitely needed to be made clear to all involved. I said she would have to find her own way there and forget about having anything to do with me on the trip.

Very quickly, the much-anticipated day approached.

Our neighbour, Dale Loewen, was also going, and we had discussed the trip together on a few occasions. Well aware of his participation, Kathy went next door and arranged to drive to the Banff barns with Dale early the following morning. It was a sombre night for me, made even more miserable by the fact that my wife, selfishly, seemed not to understand my predicament. She was upbeat and excited about the impending adventure, chatting merrily away with my turncoat neighbour.

In the gloom of the early morning, two warden trucks pulled out of Lake Louise and headed for Banff. I drove in suppressed anger by myself, trailing the other two in their truck. I caught their reflection in the headlights as they talked animatedly. I secretly hoped Kathy would regret going once things came down to the crunch and she had to keep up with the boys.

Kathy still had to explain to Gaby why she was there and not Earl. That would be interesting. I envisioned her being told to go home. Then I figured, no, she would get bucked off and have to be taken out by air ambulance, an evil thought I quickly suppressed. Maybe she would just get scared and apologize to everyone, especially me, and then go home. I was even beginning to congratulate myself on my restraint. I had certainly tried to warn her about what she was up against.

I didn't want to miss Kathy's arrival and had long since passed Dale as he dawdled to Banff. I arrived at the barns before the sun was up and found the place in organized chaos. Transportation to Ya Ha Tinda was being arranged and gear and people accounted for, all under the guidance and supervision of Banff's barn boss, Johnny Nylund.

After some delay, Dale and Kathy arrived. If Gaby was surprised to see her, he didn't show it. He casually asked her where Earl was. As she hauled out her saddle, she simply said that he had to go to a wedding, adding that her chief park warden asked her to fill in instead. Obviously, my fallback strategy hadn't worked. Maybe she would still get scared and go home, but by now I didn't think that would work either. Nobody said a thing to me—no reference to our relationship, no question about her being there at all.

Over the next three days, 10 wardens would herd 120 head of wild range horses over Snow Creek Summit and down the Cascade Fire Road to the Banff government barns, at that time located just past the airstrip. The distance was roughly 90 kilometres. The tricky part would be getting the horses off the range, which they would be reluctant to leave.

The whole trip would be a test of endurance and riding skills, trying to keep up with the herd and moving them without losing any on the way. From past experience chasing wild horses in the foothills in my younger days, I knew we would constantly be heading them off. They would be trying to circle back home through territory they knew much better than many of us did. It would be a wild ride for anyone who had not done this sort of thing before.

When we arrived at the Ya Ha Tinda Ranch, our first

test that morning was to catch a mount suitable to the task. When the ranch hands had brought the horses in, they had been able to keep the ones belonging to each park separate. That way we could ride a mount we knew. This was important, because you wanted to know what you were getting in terms of stamina and temperament for the chase ahead. No one needed a bronc or a horse that couldn't keep up. I had worked in Yoho for several years before moving to Banff and knew those horses pretty well—better, in fact, than I knew the Banff horses. I don't think Kathy really cared or was surprised when I chose one of the finest horses from the Yoho string for the coming days.

She was a tall mare with lots of fire and spirit, appropriately called Flirt. I knew Kathy had her own personal favourite, and I was just a little apprehensive when she claimed him, because he could be a handful. His name was Charcoal, and as Kathy had often reminded me, he looked like a smaller version of Fury from the old television series of the same name. According to Kathy, he was as wild as a wolf after a winter on the range and put on quite a show at being caught. I thought he had the potential to buck her off.

One of the cowboys trying to get a rope on him finally looked at Kathy and said, "Are you sure this is the one you want?" She was sure. She had ridden him many times under all kinds of conditions, particularly in Yoho's year-end gymkhana events, where you really got to know what a horse could do. He was a sure-footed, fast little quarter horse and arguably the best horse in the park. It was a good choice, and I had to admit it wasn't likely she was going home unless he bucked her off.

Although I was concerned about Kathy's safety, I was still mad, and when she threw her saddle on Charcoal I couldn't resist saying loudly, "Better be careful getting on. Remember, he dumped you last year when you were mounting." All eyes fell on me as I read their minds. They wondered why I wasn't topping Charcoal off for her. This meant riding the horse first to get the buck out of him. I said nothing more; my body language said it all.

Every cowboy and warden in spitting distance stopped what they were doing to see if there was going to be a show. I almost felt sorry for Kathy when she looked at the row of men waiting to see if she would pass the first test. It was no time to screw up, and I had pretty well declared I wasn't in her camp. But she kept her cool, and I began to remember why I married her.

"Yeah, thanks for reminding me," she calmly replied. "I better walk him some to get him settled down." She headed off for a quiet place where she could work the horse alone and not be distracted by the commotion. She was also probably looking for a stump, as she wasn't very tall—a problem when you are mounting a jumpy horse that hasn't been ridden in eight months.

Everyone got busy then, as there was still a lot to do, and the herd was getting restless. Nobody really noticed when Kathy quietly showed up, mounted and ready to ride. And what a ride! We had 120 head of horses to chase 27 kilometres to Scotch Camp, our first destination, across open country full of bush, potholes, ditches, logs and anything else that popped up. The herd was wild and full of energy, and most of the ride would be at a flat-out run. At any point, the herd could try to double back or break away, and it was our job to head them off. You could never watch your own mount, as your eyes had to be trained on the fleeing animals to anticipate their every move. Sometimes you might wind up going full blast through a dense stand of trees where low-lying branches could sweep you off. But once down, you could never catch up. It was critical to trust your mount to keep his feet and choose the best ground.

Cal Hayes, the diminutive ranch foreman, had a glint in his eye as he mounted the corral railing. "Are you ready?" he shouted. "Here they come!"

The gates swung open and the chase was on. Off we went with Johnny Nylund and Larry Gilmar leading the herd. We were all caught off guard as we madly tried to get in position to get them around the first corner and headed in the right direction. My horse was flying over the ground, pounding up the turf as we hazed a small group of Kootenay horses back to the trail. Out of the corner of my eye, I could see Kathy as she cleared a ditch, chasing a small bay. She was grinning from ear to ear as she waved at one of the cowboys helping her with a few of the more independent horses. He

Kathy Calvert at the summit of Dolomite Pass.

was grinning back, but from then on no one paid her any special attention. She was a full part of the crew, and that was all that counted now that we were on our way.

From the get-go, Johnny and Larry were at a full gallop, trying to keep ahead of the pent-up mass of energy. They were concerned about being overtaken by some of the faster animals and losing their position as leaders controlling the direction the herd would take. They rode hard, waving their arms and yelling, keeping the attention of the horses at the front on them and not on the open terrain ahead. The last thing that Johnny and Larry needed was for the riders at the back to push the horses too much or crowd them. They needn't have worried—everyone was riding pell-mell just to keep up.

Larry was an older, wily veteran of the warden service who was quite stocky in build. He was amazingly agile for a man his size and had reflexes as quick as a cat. He was the type of guy who, if you hung him from a rooftop by his boot straps, would always land on his feet.

Johnny was one of the boys from Millarville, well suited for his present position at the head of the line. When Cal Hayes retired as the ranch boss at Ya Ha Tinda, Johnny would be selected by Gaby to fill the void. He was assisted by his wife, Marie, as capable a woman as any working around horses, who helped her husband with the intricacies of running a ranch with a breeding program.

On we went, mile after bone-jarring mile, ducking and jumping whatever came our way. Soon the wranglers were working as a team, and after 20 kilometres we were able to set a steady pace to the cabin.

Scotch Camp is one of the most beautifully situated warden cabins in Banff National Park. It sits at the base of the eastern mountains overlooking the meadows and flats of the Red Deer River. It was an excellent place to hold the horses for the night before the trek over Snow Creek Summit. The grazing was good, and it was familiar territory to most of the herd.

Kathy knew most of the other wardens on the trip and was settling in comfortably and helping out with camp chores. My refusal to acknowledge her presence was getting a bit uncomfortable for me, but not at all for her. In fact, she ignored me altogether. If anyone thought this odd, nobody said a word. Before long, the cook had steaks and beans ready for the crew. The food and beer mellowed the tired riders, and soon we were reflecting on how well the day had gone. Everyone had stories of catching strays, clearing bush or surviving a nasty jump. Before long I was passing comments Kathy's way. Maybe my concerns about having a wife along were misplaced. By the time I rolled up for bed, it was as though there had never been an argument about her coming on this trip.

The next day took us over Snow Creek Summit on the old Cascade Fire Road that used to service all the warden cabins from Banff through to Scotch Camp. The road runs through some of the most beautiful country on the eastern slopes of the Rockies, but it was soon to be closed for rehabilitation. This is prime grizzly bear country, and with the advent of the helicopter the road was no longer needed as a fire access.

The horses were not particularly eager to keep going in the direction of Banff, but the country was more confined here, and it was difficult for them to make a break through the timber. They were also tired from the run the previous day and less inclined to revolt. That would change when we came to the open meadows of the summit. We were ready for them, and when we hit the high meadows, the herd was well flanked with a lead rider ahead to give direction. I rode to the side where I liked to be, apart and on my own to handle strays trying to sneak back through the bush. I had experience in deep timber and knew how to bring them back. It was a fine day; the sun shone on the newly budding willows, and there was plenty of dew on the grass. The horses cut a swath through the scrub as they let fly over the summit.

Day two ended at Windy warden cabin, on the Panther River. We had covered only 16 kilometres on the second day, because the climb to the summit was hard on the horses. We also had to watch out for their feet, which were not shod. The evening meal was quiet that night, as the final day would be the big push to get to Banff.

The next morning held the same excitement as the first day, if anything could equal that. We expected a long ride, and many of the riders were using new horses for this last push. I was not surprised when Kathy chose to ride her filly from the year before. She had been building a bond with the young horse and felt that this was the best way to re-establish that connection for the coming summer.

I agreed with her, but I knew she was taking a chance. The filly had little experience with chasing horses, and the last lap of the day would be a chase across the open airstrip to the government barns. But I had complete faith in Kathy's abilities and by now was 100 percent behind her decision to join the trip. So I was a little surprised when one of the older wardens asked me if I wanted to ride the filly in the corral first to top her off. I realized that it was vital for Kathy to have a chance to show her independence and prove her capabilities. I managed to look surprised and said, "Hell, it's her horse, let her do it."

Again, I nervously watched as she brought out the young horse and saddled her in the corral. The filly looked a bit skittish, but nothing more. Kathy mounted with assurance and rode easily around the confined space with no problem. It was good to see her so happy with the filly's performance, because I knew she had been secretly apprehensive.

Soon the outfit was on the move again for the tough 42-kilometre ride to the open meadows of the Banff airstrip and the end of the trip. I thought that the herd had settled down, resigned to returning to the parks for the summer work, but nothing is ever over until it's over. Repeatedly, small bunches of horses tried to escape, which led to some desperate riding at full gallop through the bush. The main herd had to keep moving, and it was tiring work rounding up the strays and pushing them hard to regain lost ground, but our adrenalin was still running high as challenge after challenge presented itself. We also knew that once we hit the open flats before the barns in Banff, it would be a free-for-all as we tried to contain the stampede that would ensue.

I didn't know that the event had attracted the attention of the media and the public. When we reached the airstrip, a crowd had gathered to cheer the arrival of the colourful horses. And what a spectacle it was! Over 120 horses thundered across the field with several wardens hot on their heels, following them to the waiting corrals. Cameras were flashing, and I think people were yelling. All I remember was staying with the herd and keeping them going in the general direction of the barns. Way off to the left, Kathy was riding flat out on her filly, laughing with excitement like everyone else. Suddenly, that moment in time nobody would ever forget was all over.

As we turned our horses loose and settled down, exhausted, to some beer and sandwiches, we knew the whole adventure had been a success. Reinforcements arrived to take care of the horses and parcel them out to the respective parks. The absentee Earl was there to give Kathy a hand with the Yoho horses. There wasn't room for all the animals in the Banff barns, so each outfit was trucked the rest of the way to their summer home. That didn't leave much time for socializing; quick goodbyes were dashed off as horses were sorted and loaded. Everyone who knew the animals individually pitched in, as no one wanted to take home the wrong horses. Johnny Nylund, who knew every horse's description by heart, supervised the whole thing closely.

Now on comfortable speaking terms with my wife, I wished her a good trip to Yoho and told her I would see her at home. We had had a major adventure together, one neither of us would forget. At least, I was quite sure she would never let *me* forget it. I had made it very clear I didn't want her along on the trip. It was obviously time that I accepted women in the warden service—everyone else had.

Index

Index

Acknowledgements

The author would like to acknowledge the following individuals for their helpful contributions to the book: Dave Wildman, June Mickle and Louise Kohler. In particular, I would like to thank Bob Haney, Perry Jacobson and Johnny and Marie Nylund for their critical analysis of the stories. I also wish to thank Scott Ward for his generosity in allowing me to use his splendid poem "Ya Ha Tinda Bound." I would like to thank Donny Mickle for his support and encouragement throughout the writing process and for allowing me to adapt his story of his early upbringing and his fine horse Ben. Finally, I would like to thank my wife, Kathy, for her contributions to the book, her long-standing support and her editorial critique.

About the Author

Dale Portman is a retired park warden who spent nearly 30 years working for the warden service, often involved with backcountry travel, mountain rescue and avalanche control work in Jasper, Banff, Yoho and Glacier/Revelstoke National Parks. He and his wife, Kathy Calvert, live in Cochrane, Alberta, and head to the mountains as often as possible. Dale has written two other books about his experiences working in the mountains of western Canada: *Rescue Dogs: Crime and Rescue Canines in the Canadian Rockies* and *Guardians of the Peaks: Mountain Rescue in the Canadian Rockies and Columbia Mountains,* the latter co-written with Kathy. Besides seeing new cultures in foreign lands, Dale's greatest love is for extended trips to remote parts of the Canadian Rockies, by skis, on foot or on horseback leading a couple of pack horses.

More Great Books in the Amazing Stories Series

Rescue Dogs

Crime and Rescue Canines in the Canadian Rockies

Dale Portman

(ISBN 978-1-894974-78-3)

This dramatic collection of true stories by retired park warden Dale Portman tells how dogs became the silent heroes of search and rescue and law enforcement in the Canadian Rockies, beginning with Alfie Burstrom and his canine partner, Ginger, the first certified avalanche search team in North America. Working in severe weather and challenging terrain, dogs and their handlers track missing persons, apprehend criminals and save lives at the sites of catastrophic avalanches. These stories of danger and devotion are sure to give readers an appreciation of the vital role of working dogs in Canada's mountain parks.

Visit www.heritagehouse.ca to see the entire list of books in this series.

More Great Books in the Amazing Stories Series

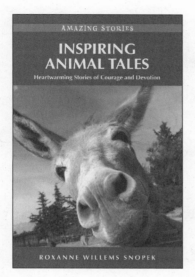

Inspiring Animal Tales

Heartwarming Stories of
Courage and Devotion

Roxanne Willems Snopek

(ISBN 978-1-894974-77-6)

Dogs, horses and other animals have long demonstrated courage, trust
and loyalty to the people in their lives, but they also inspire selfless love
in return. This touching collection of true stories shows how people and
animals come together to overcome life's challenges and find hope for
the future. From National Service Dogs that give autistic children the
gift of love and security to dedicated animal lovers who devote their
lives to rescuing and healing abused or abandoned big cats, donkeys
and parrots, the relationships portrayed in these stories are truly
heartwarming.

Visit www.heritagehouse.ca to see the entire list of books in this series.

More Great Books in the Amazing Stories Series

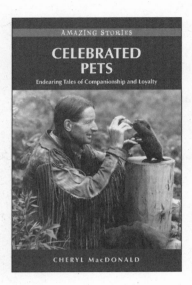

Celebrated Pets

Endearing Tales of
Companionship and Loyalty

Cheryl MacDonald

(ISBN 978-1-894974-81-3)

Throughout history, dogs, cats and other animals have served as loyal and inspiring companions. From the devoted, yet unusual relationship between Prime Minister Mackenzie King and his Irish terrier, Pat, to Emily Carr's engaging menagerie and Grey Owl's endearing Beaver People, these true tales show how pets enrich the lives of those who love them. Filled with comedy and tragedy, these unforgettable stories not only celebrate famous animals like the real Winnie-the-Pooh and Jumbo the elephant, but also the valiant dogs and horses employed in police work today.

Visit www.heritagehouse.ca to see the entire list of books in this series.